Walking Tours of Old Washington and Alexandria

Walking Tours of Old Washington and Alexandria

PAUL HOGARTH

EPM Publications, Inc.
McLean, Virginia

EPM Publications, Inc.
1003 Turkey Run Road
McLean, Virginia 22101

Printed in the United States of America
Book design by Susan Lehmann

Library of Congress Cataloging in Publication Data
Hogarth, Paul, 1917-
    Walking tours of old Washington and Alexandria.
    Includes index.
    1. Washington (D.C.)—Description—1981—Tours.
2. Walking—Washington (D.C.)—Guide-books.
3. Alexandria (Va.)—Description—Tours.
4. Walking—Virginia—Alexandria—Guide-books. I. Title.
Fl92.3.H63 1985   917.53'044   85-12907
ISBN 0-914440-85-3

Front cover: The first building in Washington, D.C., to be
designed as an art museum is the Renwick Gallery, an outstanding
example of Victorian architecture. It was designed in 1859 as the
Corcoran Gallery of Art and renamed for its architect, James
Renwick, in 1965.

Back cover: The Friendship Fire Company, the oldest group of
firefighters in Alexandria, Va., was organized in 1774 and is still
in existence. Its fire house was built in 1855.

Contents

List of Illustrations

Acknowledgments

My text is based on such a wide assortment of materials that it wouldn't be possible to acknowledge each and every source, although I have tried to do so whenever a quote or reference has been made. The more important sources include Constance McLaughlin Green's *Washington: A History of the Capital, 1860–1950* (1976); the Junior League of Washington's *City of Washington* (1977); and the following publications of the Commission of Fine Arts and HABS (Historic American Buildings Survey), *Georgetown Architecture*–Northwest Washington, Nos 5, 6, and 10 (1970); *The Mansions of Massachusetts Avenue,* Volumes 1 and 2 (1977–1978). References to European travelers' impressions were found in Max Berger's *The British Traveler in America, 1836–1860* (1943); Richard L. Rapson's *Britons View America 1860–1935* (1971) and Marc Pachter's *Abroad in America: Visitors to the New Nation, 1776–1914* (1976). Other sources were the memoirs, reminiscences, and autobiographical works published by celebrated Washington hostesses, notably Evalyn Walsh McLean's *Father Struck It Rich* (1936); Countess Marguerite Cassini's *Never a Dull Moment* (1956), and Alice Hogue's *Cissy Patterson* (1966). To these author's researches and comments I am indebted.

I am grateful to the curators and docents who contributed their knowledge and time to the book in manuscript: in particular Robert Lyle of the Georgetown Regional Library; Emily Eig of *Traceries;* Elizabeth Miller of the Columbia Historical Society; Diane Bechtol of the Alexandria Tourist Council.

I should like to thank several Washingtonians whose hospitality helped sustain me during my stay in the city. These are too numerous to cite in full, but I do owe a special debt to Caroline Despard of *Smithsonian;* Alan Fern, Director of Special Collections, Library of Congress; Ira Glackens; Dr. Richard Howland, formerly of the Smithsonian Institution, for his generous and helpful criticism of the manuscript; and the inimitable John Prince, whose love for Georgetown enabled him to take me on his own walking tour.

I should also like to thank Mr. and Mrs. Armistead Peter, III, and Mrs. Peter Belin for their kindness in allowing me to depict their respective houses, Tudor Place and Evermay; the National Register of Historic Places and William Murtagh, whose files provided such extensive background information; the Columbia Historical Society and Perry Fisher, for helpful advice and research facilities; the Alexandria Public Library Historical Collection at Lloyd House and Mrs. Lee DeRoche; the Peabody Room, Georgetown Public Library, and Miss Mathilda Williams; the Washingtonia Room, Martin Luther King Library, and J. R. F. Key; the Library of the Office of Community Services, Washington Metropolitan Transit Authority (Metro), and Librarian John Duval; Rae Koch, site historian, Old Stone House; the Pennsylvania Avenue Development Corporation and Ms. Rita Abraham; and last but not least, my son Toby Hogarth, whose help as research assistant extraordinary played such a vital part.

P.H.

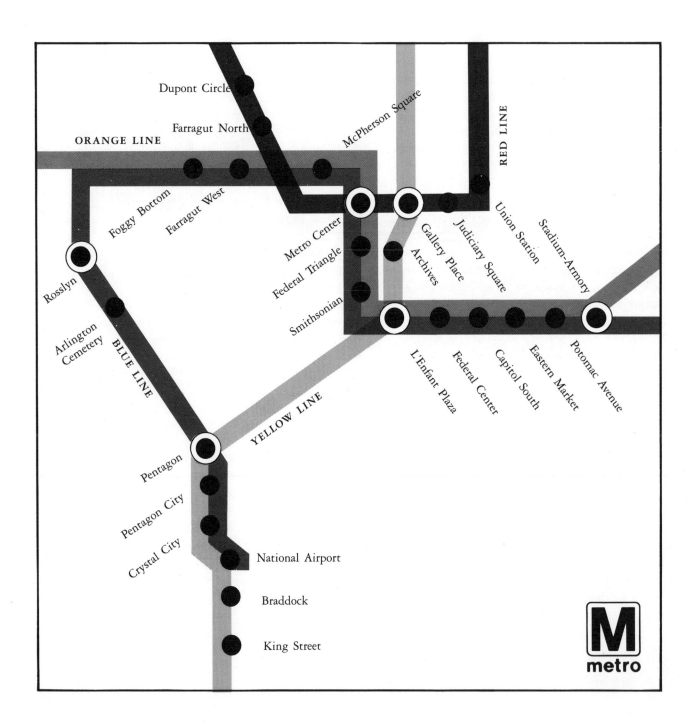

Dupont Circle

Farragut North

McPherson Square

RED LINE

ORANGE LINE

Foggy Bottom

Farragut West

Metro Center

Federal Triangle

Smithsonian

Gallery Place

Judiciary Square

Archives

Union Station

Stadium-Armory

Rosslyn

Arlington
Cemetery

BLUE LINE

L'Enfant Plaza

Federal Center

Capitol South

Eastern Market

Potomac Avenue

YELLOW LINE

Pentagon

Pentagon City

Crystal City

National Airport

Braddock

King Street

M metro

Getting Around

I have restricted my Washington to seven walks, resisting temptations to include the museums and galleries, the monuments and memorials of the Mall. The Tourmobile Mall trip is a convenient and inexpensive way of meeting this requirement. I felt there was a greater need for an artist's discovery of a Washington that usually gets left out. So I have selected the more historically fascinating neighborhoods, using outstanding or unusual examples of architecture to bring alive a city much different from anything you might have expected.

Washington is divided into two parts, the original city envisaged by L'Enfant and now completely developed; plus a total of some twenty-five sections located outside his plan, which developed in the late nineteenth century and the early twentieth century. Here we are concerned with parts of both—the White House neighborhood, Downtown and Capitol Hill in L'Enfant's city, and historic Georgetown, which predates Washington by more than half a century; and the mansions of Massachusetts Avenue, built between 1870 and 1920. Five tours through these sections enable us to appreciate a wide range of historical associations.

Two additional tours include the nearby historic port of Old Alexandria, Virginia, and equally historic Mount Vernon. Alexandria was a thriving port in colonial times and retains much of its original residential atmosphere. No visit to the Federal City is complete without seeing Mount Vernon, the former residence and estate of George Washington.

Finding your way around Washington is easy. The city is divided into four quadrants or areas—Northwest, Southwest, Northeast, and Southeast—with the Capitol at the center. All streets within each quadrant bear the designation of that quadrant; for example, 2017 I Street, NW, is located in the northwest part of the city. This is important to remember, because there is a 2017 I Street in more than one area. Numbered streets run north and south, lettered streets east and west. Avenues (named after states in the nation) cross these at angles, and the major avenues radiate from the Capitol like the spokes of a gigantic wheel.

Although it is possible to start at any point on the walks, the tours are sometimes difficult to drive because of one-way streets, heavy traffic, and severely limited on-street parking. Drive (if you must) to the starting point of a tour and leave your vehicle in a lot or garage, or better still take the Metro or even Metrobus. Washington's new rapid transit system, Metro, is good to ride and serves three of the walking tours. But note that the Metro operates Monday through Saturday 6:00 A.M.–12:00 MIDNIGHT and Sunday 10:00 A.M.–6:00 P.M. Free transfers, permitting you to board Metrobuses outside Metro stations, are available at no extra charge. Metro stations are easily spotted by their distinctive bronze pylons with the big white *M*. A map of the Metro system as of this writing can be found on page 8.

Metrobus, on the other hand, serves *all* the walking tours. Ask for a free map of the system at any Visitor Information Center, or at your hotel. Route information is given for each tour. For route and schedule information, telephone the Metropolitan Transit Authority (202)637-2437.

Taxicabs are available during the day but vanish during rush hours and wet weather. Washington cab fares, by the way, are determined by a zone system whereby the city is divided into regions and charges are calculated according to boundaries crossed. No reduced group rates apply except where two or more passengers enter and leave the cab at the same points.

Although Washington's weather is generally good, it has always aroused unfavorable comment from travelers. Spring is sometimes mild and sometimes not; this hasn't changed since Dickens's first visit in March 1841. "One day, it is hot summer," he wrote, "without a breath of air; the next, twenty degrees below freezing, with a wind blowing that cuts your skin like steel." The best times to visit Washington are April through June, or September through October, usually fine periods. July and August are usually extremely hot and humid. Temperatures soar into the nineties, although air conditioning does bring relief in museums and buses.

Unless you plan to stay at least four days, you won't have time to walk all seven tours. But regardless of how long your visit is, start the first day with an early morning tour of the *White House Neighborhood*. Proceed next to Capitol Hill for a quick look at the U.S. Capitol and to view the distant Mall and the Washington Monument. After lunch in the Capitol's café-restaurant, take the *Downtown Tour*.

A full day, the second, should be devoted to the *Mansions of Massachusetts Avenue* and after lunch, *Georgetown*. These are a must for those who like strolling along shady streets and looking at—and in—fine old houses and antique shops.

A trip into Virginia on the third day will take you back to colonial days and the private world of George Washington. In the morning, a visit to Mount Vernon should take about three hours. In the afternoon, see *Old Alexandria*; if time allows, you should also dine here.

Remaining time might be spent looking at the monuments, memorials, and historic buildings of the Mall, by Tourmobile. This comfortable bus makes the city's major sites of interest in about an hour, and includes the following: the White House, Lincoln Memorial, Jefferson Memorial, U.S. Capitol, Smithsonian Institution Building, National Museum of American History, Museum of Natural History, National Gallery of Art, Bureau of Engraving and Printing, Arlington Cemetery Visitors' Center, Washington Monument.

Each of the seven walking tours in this book begins with a map showing all the buildings I have drawn, with numbers keyed to the text. Museums and other places of interest not illustrated are indicated in the text and on the maps by an asterisk. The arrows indicate the direction in which I walked (which could be reversed should you wish to begin your walk at the opposite end). Top of the page is north.

Much of the factual information in my book has been, and is, subject to change. Visitors to historical sites should check on times of opening and closing and on admission charges. In some cases, too, continuing restoration on sites may have altered the appearance of a building since it was drawn or described here.

The White House Neighborhood

The White House

Distance: 2 miles. Time: 2 to 3 hours, depending on how many historic buildings are visited. Metro: McPherson Square (Vermont and I). Metrobus: 30, 32, 34, 36, and all 80s to Lafayette Park. Parking: commercial lots to north along H, I, and K Streets, NW.

The White House neighborhood is an impressive start to your visit to the nation's capital. Its epicenter, historic Lafayette Square, was for many years the hub of the country's social and political life. Originally part of the White House grounds and known as "Presidents' Square," it was named for the Marquis de Lafayette after his official visit of 1824. The neighborhood soon became the location for the republican counterpart of court residences. It can claim a nucleus of historic mansions and public buildings, which have survived, some with their original furnishings, because of an imaginative restoration project initiated by President John F. Kennedy.

The White House itself, The Octagon, Blair House, Decatur House, St. John's Church, Madison House, and the Tayloe-Cameron House take us back to the days of the administrations of James Monroe

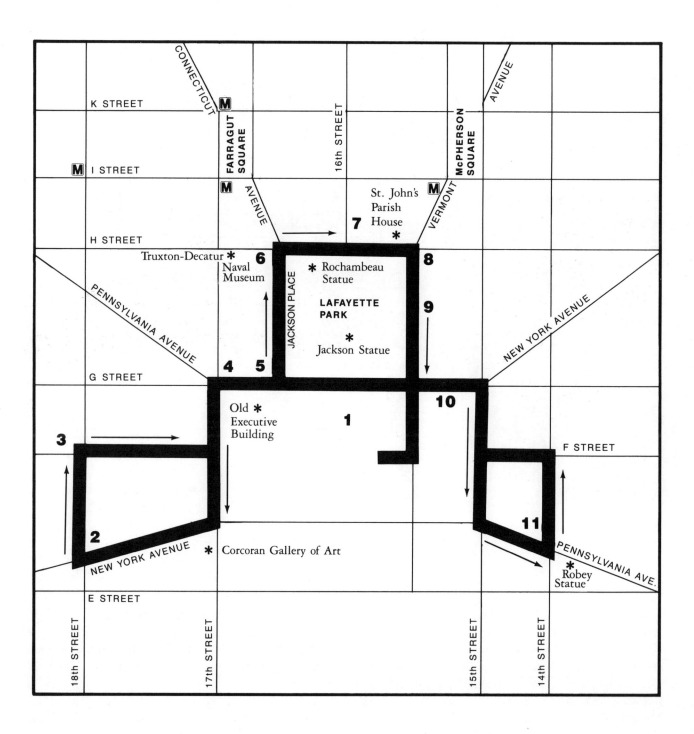

K STREET

CONNECTICUT

M

I STREET

FARRAGUT SQUARE

M

16th STREET

McPHERSON SQUARE

AVENUE

H STREET

AVENUE

St. John's Parish House

VERMONT

M

7

*

Truxton-Decatur *

6

* Rochambeau Statue

8

Naval Museum

LAFAYETTE PARK

9

PENNSYLVANIA AVENUE

JACKSON PLACE

NEW YORK AVENUE

G STREET

4 5

* Jackson Statue

Old *
Executive
Building

1

10

3

F STREET

2

NEW YORK AVENUE

* Corcoran Gallery of Art

11

PENNSYLVANIA AVE.

* Robey Statue

E STREET

18th STREET

17th STREET

15th STREET

14th STREET

(1817–1825), John Quincy Adams (1825–1829), and Andrew Jackson (1829–1837). The Renwick Gallery (Old Corcoran Art Gallery), St. John's Parish Building (Old British Embassy), and the Willard Hotel reflect the more flamboyant Gilded Age (1865–1896).

Much of the social and political life of the young and bustling Federal city centered on Lafayette Square and adjacent F and G Streets, west of 17th Street. St. John's Church was *the* fashionable church, and every Sunday the wealthy and influential could be seen in their finest walking down the street through Lafayette Square to St. John's. "Lafayette Square," wrote Henry Adams, "*was* society."

The neighborhood is especially rich in the wide range of its historical associations. Its main attraction, the elegant White House, was the first of the capital's public buildings to be completed, and has been the residence of every President except George Washington. The Octagon served as the executive mansion after the White House was burned by the British during the War of 1812. At Blair House, during the occupancy of Montgomery Blair, Postmaster-General in Lincoln's cabinet, Robert E. Lee was offered command of the Union army. Lee rejected the offer and accepted the command of the forces of the Confederacy. Decatur House, briefly the home of Commodore Stephen Decatur, the ill-starred naval hero, and his beautiful wife, was the scene of many entertainments and historic events, as was the Richard Cutts House, where Dolley Madison lived from 1828 until her death in 1849; the Cutts House was also lived in by President Martin Van Buren. Dolley, who served as White House hostess for President Thomas Jefferson and as First Lady during the administration of her husband, James Madison, made the house a great political salon. Civil War buffs will be interested to learn that during the greater part of that war the Army of the Potomac occupied the house as headquarters. The nearby Tayloe House was occupied by a host of distinguished politicians, including Senator Marcus Hanna, Republican boss and millionaire.

All in all, it isn't difficult to imagine the manners and customs, costumes and balls that took place before the turn of the century when Connecticut Avenue and K Street, and later Massachusetts Avenue, replaced the White House neighborhood as Washington's most fashionable area.

The White House

1600 Pennsylvania Avenue, NW. A National Historic Landmark. Telephone: (202)456-1414. Metro: McPherson Square (Vermont and I). Metrobus: 30, 32, 34, 36, and all 80s to Lafayette Park. Tourmobile to the Ellipse. Open Tuesday through Saturday 10:00 A.M.–12:00 NOON. From Memorial Day to Labor Day tickets with a designated touring time may be obtained on the Ellipse; available on a first-come, first-served basis the day of the tour. Visitor entrance at East Gate, East Executive Avenue (between Pennsylvania Avenue and Alexander Hamilton Place, NW). Closed Thanksgiving and Christmas. Free. Time: 15–20 minutes. Visitors with a physical handicap should go directly to the East Gate for prompt admittance.

The **White House (1)** was built between 1792 and 1800 on a site selected by Pierre Charles L'Enfant and George Washington. It was known as the President's House or the President's Palace until it was painted white in 1798.

Since that time the White House has grown from a modest Georgian house to an elegant edifice of fifty-four rooms and sixteen bathrooms exclusive of office space. Its first occupants were President and Mrs. John Adams, who moved into the unfinished house in November 1800. It was not completely finished until almost ten years later. Then came the War of 1812.

On August 24, 1814, a British expeditionary force landed at Chesapeake Bay, marched on Washington, and burned the city in retaliation for the destruction of public buildings in Canada. Madison, who had made no plans for defending the capital, borrowed a pair of dueling pistols and drove out to Bladensburg, Maryland. But when the British fired their new Congreve rockets, mules and militia stampeded, and the battle was lost. The sixty-three-year-old President drove off in the opposite direction, and when somebody found a wagon, Dolley, his indomitable First Lady, gallantly assisted by the New York banker, Jacob Barker, and Charles Carroll, loaded it with the White House silver, Gilbert Stuart's full-length portrait of George Washington, four boxes of official papers, a few precious books, a clock, and some red velvet curtains. Everything else was lost after Admiral Sir George Cockburn ordered burning balls of pitch to be shot through the windows. Only a violent rainstorm that night prevented the destruction of the entire city.

The White House embodies the ambitions of two

distinguished architects. James Hoban (c. 1762–1831), a young Irishman practicing in Charleston, South Carolina, had in mind Leinster House, the celebrated Dublin *palazzo* of the aristocratic Fitzgerald family (now the senate of Ireland's parliament), when he prepared his design. Although Hoban supervised both the original construction and reconstruction after Cockburn's exploit, Benjamin Latrobe (1764–1820), an Englishman who came to America in 1796 to become its first great architect, added later refinements, notably the east and west terraces. Hoban also supervised the construction of the north portico facing Lafayette Park, which was built in 1829 after a design by Latrobe.

To give even a sampling of the many historic movements and occasions that have taken place within the walls of the White House would fill a book of many pages. Every President since John Adams has lived here, entertaining and receiving a constant stream of famous and distinguished visitors, while working and worrying over affairs of great and momentous concern.

During the height of the tourist season, you may have to wait in line for one hour, possibly longer, to be admitted. Once inside visitors may view the rooms at their own pace; tour officials are available to answer questions. One good tip: Write or visit your Senator or Congressman to see if you can arrange to join the more leisurely early morning VIP tour at 8:00 A.M. As most visitors will have to be content with the regular tour, an excellent book *The White House, An Historical Guide* (White House Historical Association, $3.75 paperback) is recommended for those interested in a detailed permanent account of the history, associations, and furnishings.

The five state rooms on the tour, beginning with the East Room and extending through the Green, Blue, and Red Rooms, and finally, the State Dining Room, are actually the most important to both the VIP and the regular tourist.

The grandest and largest of them all, the East Room, was planned by Hoban as a public reception room, which it still is. It is also the most historic. Abigail Adams on her arrival found most of the executive mansion unplastered; she hung out the family wash in the unfinished room. Seven Presidents have lain in state here including, Lincoln, McKinley, and Kennedy. On the east wall is the most celebrated portrait in the White House, Gilbert Stuart's Washington, the very one Dolley Madison saved.

The handsome Green Room served a variety of purposes for the early Presidents. Jefferson used it as his personal dining room. Madison used it as a sitting room adjoining the East Room, where his cabinet met. During the Monroe administration it was a card room. John Quincy Adams made it a green drawing room, which it has remained.

The oval Blue Room is the most elegant room in the White House and reflects the Francophile taste of President Monroe, who installed the superb French Empire gilded wood furniture in order to give the White House a more stately atmosphere. The color blue was first used in the room during the Van Buren administration (1837–1841). The Blue Room is often used by the President to receive guests at state dinners and receptions. Portraits in the room include Jefferson by Rembrandt Peale, John Adams by John Trumbull, and John Tyler by G.P.A. Healy.

The Red Room, third of the sitting rooms or parlors, is used for small receptions. John Adams used it as a breakfast room; later Presidents used it as a music room. It is magnificently decorated in the American Empire style of 1810–1830. Walls are covered with a red satin fabric with a gold scroll border. The furniture is upholstered in the same fabric and the draperies are of gold satin with red damask valances.

Next is the State Dining Room. Originally smaller, it once adjoined the grand staircase. It was enlarged in 1902 by McKim, Mead and White on the orders of Theodore Roosevelt, who also had the lavish English oak paneling put in, as well as the flamboyant fireplace of carved buffalo heads, reminders of his beloved West.

Continue west on Pennsylvania Avenue past the Old Executive Office Building, a colossal Victorian structure on the corner of 17th Street and Pennsylvania Avenue. Turn left on 17th, then right on New York Avenue to our next stop, The Octagon.

The Octagon

1799 New York Avenue, NW. A National Historic Landmark owned by the American Institute of Architects. Telephone: (202)638-3105. Metro: Farragut West (18th and I). Open Tuesday through Friday 10:00 A.M.–4:00 P.M.; Saturday and Sunday 1:00–4:00 P.M. Closed Thanksgiving, Christmas, New Year's Day and Easter. Free guided tour. Time 20–25 minutes.

The Octagon

On the northwest corner of 18th Street and New York Avenue, three blocks southwest of the Renwick Gallery is **The Octagon** (2), a Federal mansion of exceptional interest. Actually a hexagon, it was built between 1798 and 1800 to the designs of William Thornton (1759–1828) for Colonel John Tayloe III, famous for his wealth and blooded horses. The house served as the President's mansion after the British burned the White House. Madison ratified the Treaty of Ghent here on February 17, 1815, finally establishing peace with England.

In later years, after the house was used as a girl's school, it sank steadily into decay until 1899 when the American Institute of Architects came to the rescue, restored the historic old house, and made it part of its national headquarters.

Coade stone mantels in the drawing room and living room were imported from England *c.* 1799. The material from which the mantels are composed is an earthenware substance made from a formula which is now lost. The beautifully decorated mantels are original to the house; if anything were to happen to them they could never be reconstructed.

The stove, located in the entryway, is original to the house. It was one of the earliest coal-burning stoves in Washington. A tunnel, now mostly filled in, runs under the house, probably under 18th Street. The tunnel's use is a matter of speculation; one theory is that it was used to store coal, which was expensive in those days.

Continue now up 18th to F Street. On the southeast corner of 18th and F Streets is our next stop, the Ringgold-Carroll or Marshall House.

Ringgold-Carroll House

Ringgold-Carroll House

1801 F Street, NW. A National Historic Landmark. Private residence, not open to the public.

The **Ringgold-Carroll House (3)**, known also as the Marshall or Bacon House, was built in 1825 by Tench Ringgold, a marshal of the District of Columbia who served on the three-man committee to supervise restoration of public buildings after the British sacked the capital. The house was a center of social activity for leading judges and prominent lawyers. The celebrated Chief Justice John Marshall boarded with Ringgold during the years 1832–1833. The tall, loose-limbed Virginian was not only a legal genius but a great wit, as fast with a quip as he was deliberate in judgment. Virginius Dabney describes the occasion on which Marshall was challenged in a Philadelphia club to use the word *paradox* in verse. He glanced through the door and saw several convivial Kentuckians and at once came up with:

In the Blue Grass region
A "paradox" was born,
The corn was full of kernels
And the "colonels" full of corn.

In 1835 the house was sold to William Thomas Carroll, grandson of Charles Carroll who served for many years as clerk of the Supreme Court. He was one of the founders of the law department at George Washington University. After Mrs. Carroll's death in 1897 the house was purchased by another legal bigwig, Chief Justice Melville Fuller, one of the founders of the Columbia Historical Society.

Although much altered throughout its history, this splendid old mansion reflects an era of symmetry and grace. It is almost square in plan, and was originally two stories plus a ground floor in height, with Flemish bond brickwork. The present entrance on the ground floor of the F Street side, with stairs ascending to the second or main floor, and the top floor, were added by Jules Henri de Sibour (1872–1938) when the Countess of Yarmouth (later Mrs. Geoffry Whitney and Mrs. Thaw) owned the house between 1911 and 1918.

Continue eastward down F Street toward the vast gray bulk of the **Old Executive Office Building***, Pennsylvania Avenue at 17th Street. Likewise a National Historic Landmark, it is not generally open to the public except by special permit. Second Empire in style, this massive monumental edifice (known for some years as the world's largest office block) was designed by Alfred Butt Mullett and built between 1871 and 1881 as the Departments of State, War, and Navy Building. Six stories high, with purple-gray Virginia granite walls and mauve-slated mansard roofs laid in complex patterns, it is "the quintessence," to quote historian Nancy Taylor, "of vigorous superscaled Victorian architecture." Notice the sculptured north pediment, which faces Pennsylvania Avenue. Designed *c.* 1884 by Richard von Ezdorf, this elaborate grouping of classical military emblems symbolizing war evokes the strength and stability of the Republic.

The interior is even more extraordinary. Two miles of grandiose corridors and ten acres of office and library space were designed by the indefatigable Von Ezdorf (one is not surprised to learn he was an Austro-Venetian aristocrat) in the style of a Venetian *palazzo*, with exquisitely handmade doors, gas-lit chandeliers, skylights, and domes over huge spiraling stairways that sweep around from floor to floor.

Opposite the Old Executive Office Building on Pennsylvania Avenue is the Renwick Gallery, our next stop.

Renwick Gallery

Pennsylvania Avenue at 17th Street, NW. A National Historic Landmark owned by the Smithsonian Institution. Telephone: (202)357-2700. Metro: Farragut West (17th and I). Open daily 10:00 A.M.–5:30 P.M. Closed Christmas. Free. Guided tours by appointment only; call (202)357-3111. Time: 15–20 minutes.

Designed in 1859 as the Corcoran Gallery of Art to house the art collection of banker William Wilson Corcoran (1798–1888), the **Renwick Gallery (4)** was the first building in Washington to be designed as an art museum. It was named for its architect, James Renwick (1818–1895), when the building was transferred by the Federal government to the

Renwick Gallery

Smithsonian Institution in 1965. Renwick, the greatest American exponent of the Gothic Revival style, turned to the French Empire style to design the building, the first erected in that style in the United States, and an outstanding example of Victorian architecture.

Shortly after the building's completion, the Civil War broke out; and Corcoran, a Confederate sympathizer, promptly exiled himself to Paris for the duration. The Union army, hungry for space, took over the building, first as a temporary hospital and then as headquarters for the quartermaster-general's corps. The gallery was returned to Corcoran in 1869, when restoration of its original design began. By this time, however, Corcoran's collection, swollen by purchases made during his exile, had outgrown the building. In 1897 his pictures were moved to the present Corcoran Gallery of Art, at 17th Street and New York Avenue.

Between 1884 and 1888, improvements were

made to the exterior. On Pennsylvania Avenue the facade was embellished with pilasters and foliated capitals. Wreaths and Corcoran's monogram, as well as the endearing inscription, "Dedicated to Art," were added on the entablature. The crowning pediment is enlivened by a bronze portrait medallion of Corcoran (1879–1884, Moses Ezekiel). Notice too the central pavilion's great mansard roof, fringed with ornamented iron railings. And last, but certainly not least, note the niches on the west facade that contain figures of Rubens and Murill (1879–1884, Moses Ezekiel), which are replicas of two of the eleven figures of famous masters that stood here until 1897.

Under the direction of the National Museum of American Art, the interior has been refurnished in the styles of the 1860s and 1870s. The paintings in the Grand Salon and the Octagon Room are hung as they were in Corcoran's day—in massive gold frames in two and three rows on wine red walls.

Blair House

1651 Pennsylvania Avenue, NW. A National Historic Landmark. Not open to the public.

Together with the adjacent Lee House (c. 1860), historic **Blair House (5)** now serves as the President's guest house for visiting heads of state. Built in 1824 by Dr. Joseph Lovell, a scion of the Lovells of Massachusetts and Surgeon-General of the Army, Blair House, when designed, was the mirror-reversed duplicate of the Ringgold-Carroll House. After Lovell's death in 1836, Francis Preston Blair, Sr., who came from Kentucky to join Jackson's "kitchen cabinet" and who amassed his wealth through real estate and by publishing the *Washington Globe*, acquired the house. The elegant old house was continuously owned by Blair descendants until 1942 and has at various times been leased to distinguished occupants. George Bancroft (1800–1891), "father of American history" and Secretary of the Navy under Polk, lived here from 1845 through 1846, while he established the United States Naval Academy in Annapolis, Maryland.

The Blairs returned to the house in the 1850s, and the mansion became famous as a place where complicated political deals were worked out—a reputation the house still enjoys. John C. Calhoun, Jefferson Davis, Daniel Webster, and Henry Clay were frequent visitors in the years before the Civil War. William Tecumseh Sherman, who later put Atlanta to the torch, was married here in 1850. Montgomery Blair, attorney for Dred Scott, a famous slave in America who was freed after many years of indecision, lived here in 1857. Later Blair served as Postmaster-General under Lincoln and originated the International Postal Union. Montgomery and his father, Francis, were confidants of Lincoln and during the Civil War many vital decisions were made in the house. In one of the front rooms, Robert E. Lee was offered command of the Union armies, and Lincoln frequently dropped in while on his walks about the neighborhood. It was here, in 1861, that Navy Captain David Glasgow Farragut ("Damn the torpedoes—full speed ahead!") was told he was to command the Union attack on New Orleans.

More recently, Harry Truman and his family lived here from 1948 to 1951, while the White House was undergoing extensive repairs. It was here on the sidewalk, on November 1, 1950, that an attempt was made on Truman's life. The President escaped injury but one of his White House guards, Leslie Coffelt, was killed. The plaque on the fence commemorates Coffelt's bravery.

Continue east toward Lafayette Square. Before turning left on Jackson Place stop to admire the statue of Andrew Jackson (1853, Clark Mills), which faces the White House in Lafayette Square. Jackson, who stopped Cockburn from burning down New Orleans, is commemorated as he appeared while reviewing his troops. Grouped around the simple granite pedestal are four cannons captured in Pensacola, Florida.

Now proceed north on Jackson Place. At the southwest corner note the dramatic statue of Comte de Rochambeau (1902, Ferdinand Hamar), who brought a force of six thousand seasoned French troops to join Washington for the Yorktown victory that resulted in the surrender of Lord Cornwallis's army. The impressive facades of several imposing old mansions (now government offices) will certainly draw your attention as we approach our next stop, Decatur House.

Blair House

Decatur House

748 Jackson Place, NW. Telephone: (202)673-4030. A National Historic Landmark owned by the National Trust for Historic Preservation. Open Tuesday through Friday 10:00 A.M.–2:00 P.M.; Saturday and Sunday 12:00 NOON–4:00 P.M. Closed Thanksgiving, Christmas, New Year's Day, and Easter. Free for National Trust members; $2.00 for adults, $1.00 for students and senior citizens. Guided tour. Time: 30 minutes.

On the northwest corner of Lafayette Square is one of the most historic mansions in Washington, **Decatur House (6)**, built by the American naval hero Commodore Stephen Decatur (1779–1820) between 1818 and 1819 with the prize money he had won for

his many daring victories over the Barbary pirates and the British in the War of 1812. In 1816 Decatur and his beautiful young wife, Susan, came to Washington where the commodore was wined and dined as the nation's greatest naval hero since John Paul Jones.

Designed by Latrobe to evoke the neoclassical spirit of the Philadelphia houses Decatur loved, the house was barely finished before Decatur fell on March 22, 1820, fatally wounded in a duel by the bullet of an old enemy, Commodore James Barron of Norfolk. Barron had been suspended from the navy

Decatur House

for five years without pay for surrendering the *Chesapeake* to the British in 1807 and blamed Decatur for damaging his career. Flags were flown at half-mast and the funeral cortege passed along Pennsylvania Avenue, where thousands stood in mourning. Legend has it that the grief-stricken Susan, who lived in the house briefly after Decatur's death, can still be heard weeping for her lost husband. She moved to Georgetown, where she lived until her death in 1860. (See page 95.)

The house was a center of political, social, and diplomatic intrigue under a succession of dis-

tinguished owners and tenants. Shortly after the Decatur tragedy, it was leased to the Russian Minister and became the Russian legation. John Gadsby, the celebrated innkeeper (see page 124), bought the house in 1836 and entertained Washington society. Three Secretaries of State lived here—"Handsome Harry" Clay, Martin Van Buren, Andrew Jackson's right-hand man, and Edward Livingston—and following them, the Civil War general Edward F. Beale. The house remained in the Beale family for eighty-five years until Marie Beale gave it to the National Trust in 1956.

Adorned in its later years with Victorian embellishments, the outside of the house has been restored to its pure Federal style, using Latrobe's original plans (now in the Library of Congress). Likewise, the first floor has been restored to its original Federal style at the time the Decaturs lived in the house. The second floor, however, has been furnished in the Victorian style of General Beale's ownership. By day, Decatur House is a museum. By night, however, with its chandeliers ablaze, the house flourishes once more as a gracious venue for receptions given by embassies and cultural organizations.

The house is filled with many beautiful pieces of furniture, paintings, and historical memorabilia—most notable are the Fitzhugh china and the Truxton Urn. The latter was presented at Lloyd's Coffee House, London, to Captain Thomas Truxton (a relative of Susan Decatur), of the U.S. frigate *Constellation*, for his action in taking the French frigate *L'Insurgente* off Nevis on February 9, 1799, during the shooting war between French and American warships in the West Indies. There are also documents of state signed by President Monroe, General Grant, and James C. Blaine, and much, much more.

Now cross H Street and turn left into 16th Street. At the southwestern corner is our next stop, St. John's Episcopal Church.

St. John's Episcopal Church

16th and H Streets, NW. A National Historic Landmark. Telephone: (202)347-8766. Open daily 8:00 A.M.–4:00 P.M. Sunday services 8:00 A.M., 9:00 A.M., and 11:00 A.M. Free guided tour on Sunday after the last service; tours by appointment Monday-Saturday. Time: 15 minutes.

Here, at the north end of Lafayette Square, is one of the finest Classical style churches in the United States, **St. John's Episcopal Church (7)**. This historic church was the second building to be erected on the square and was built between 1815 and 1816 after a rectangular plan by Latrobe. Simplicity characterizes the design. Latrobe was so proud of it that he refused to accept a fee. "I have," he wrote to his son Henry in 1816, "just completed a church that made many Washingtonians religious who have not been religious before." Latrobe himself was the first organist and choirmaster.

The church was enlarged in 1822. A Doric-columned Greek porch was added according to stage two of Latrobe's plan, and, in spite of many later alterations and enlargements, the exterior of the church has since remained essentially unchanged. Before Latrobe left England in 1795, he may have seen Sir John Soane's revolutionary work at the Bank of England (1788–1808). This, as Nikolaus Pevsner states, would account for the most striking innovations—for instance, the exquisite cupola and lantern. An unusual feature is the Victorian character of the stained glass, which is beautiful or superfluous, depending on how you look at your churches. The rows of white pews, which include the President's pew (Pew 54) where every President of the United States since Madison has sat, complete the perfect picture of gracious churchgoing.

Adjacent to the church is **St. John's Parish House***, at 1525 H Street, NW. Built between 1822 and 1836 by Matthew St. Clair Clark, clerk of the House of Representatives, the house was a hive of British diplomatic activity between 1842 and 1852. In 1842 it was occupied by Lord Alexander Baring Ashburton, the portly British minister sent to Washington to eliminate several irritating bones of contention, notably the northwestern boundary dispute. Before leaving England, his lordship had written to Daniel Webster, then Secretary of State, to procure a suitable house for his use.

Ashburton was no stranger to the United States, having previously represented his father's business interests in Philadelphia. He had married Anne Louise Bingham, eldest daughter of Senator Bingham of Pennsylvania. Like the equally portly Webster, Ashburton was addicted to the pleasures of the table, firmly believing that *haute cuisine* was the first step in smoothing out difficulties between nations.

Thereupon, the two statesmen engaged in a contest. One night they had Parisian potages, ragouts, and casseroles at Ashburton's house, and the next night they feasted on New Jersey oysters, Maryland crabs, and Chesapeake ducks at Webster's house (1611 H Street). Naturally, all this gourmandizing, together with their great esteem for one another, made for successful negotiation, and the Canadian boundary dispute was satisfactorily settled. After Ashburton's tenure, the house was acquired by Great Britain and served as the British legation from 1849 to 1852.

Paul HOGARTH
St Johns Church
Lafayette Square

23

Cutts-Madison House

Cutts-Madison House

1520 H Street, NW. A National Historic Landmark. Federal Judiciary Center, not open to the public.

Next stop on our clockwise progression around Lafayette Square is the **Cutts-Madison House (8)** built in 1820 by Richard Cutts, Congressman from Massachusetts and husband of Anne Payne, Dolley Madison's sister. This dignified old house was second only to the White House as a setting for social and political intrigue. After the death of her husband, James Madison, the ever-popular Dolley moved here in 1836 and entertained in lavish style. Although born a Quaker, she enjoyed playing cards for money, took snuff, used rouge, and wore extravagant clothes.

After Dolley Madison's death in 1849, John C. Crittenden, Attorney General under the Taylor administration (1849–1850) and William C. Preston, a Senator from South Carolina, lived in the house. Later, naval hero Commodore Charles Wilkes resided here. It was Wilkes who seized the British vessel *Trent* in November 1861, more than seven months after the outbreak of the Civil War, and arrested the Confederate commissioners, James M. Mason of Virginia and John Slidell of Louisiana, while they were crossing the Atlantic to represent the Southern cause in Europe. During the war itself, the Army of the Potomac occupied the house, which was also the residence of George Brinton McClellan, at the time commander-in-chief of the Union army, until 1862.

Later in the nineteenth century, the Cutts-Madison House and the adjacent Tayloe House were acquired by the Cosmos Club, a private club founded in 1878 to recognize men distinguished in the arts and sciences. The club is now on Massachusetts Avenue (see page 70). Both houses are now Federal government offices.

Tayloe House

Tayloe House

21 Madison Place, NW. A National Historic Landmark. Not open to the public.

Walk a few steps farther to pause and view the **Tayloe House (9)**, a handsome mansion of the Federal era, built by Benjamin Ogle Tayloe in 1828. Benjamin, the second son of John Tayloe, the owner of Octagon House, followed his father's lead and collected fine furniture, paintings, and objets d'art from his world travels. He was an urbane host and his house became a celebrated port of call for diplomats and foreign notables visiting the capital—so much so, that it was dubbed "The Little White House."

After Tayloe's death in 1868, the house was occupied by Admiral Hiram Paulding, McKinley's Vice President Garret C. Hobart, James D. Cameron, and Senator Marcus Hanna. President-maker Hanna was certainly the most colorful. Gone were the days of Tayloe's gracious socializing. Hanna entertained his guests at enormous breakfasts of corned-beef hash. "Uncle Mark," as he was nicknamed, was a remarkable politician. His biggest triumph was organizing the election of McKinley against the Presidential candidate of the Silver Democrats, popular William Jennings Bryan. In doing so, he staged a parade in New York in which a hundred and fifty thousand businessmen, bankers, lawyers, and clergymen stomped up Broadway wearing top hats and swallow-tailed coats. He sent out a hundred million pieces of campaign literature, tons of gold pieces of elephants, gold hats, *and* golden sheaves of wheat. Hanna believed that the Federal government existed primarily to help business. And after that, business could help the rest of the country. Yet he was one of the first big industrialists to sign a union contract.

25

Treasury Building

1500 Pennsylvania Avenue, NW. Telephone: (202)566-5221. A National Historic Landmark. Entrance on East Executive Avenue opposite visitor entrance to the White House. Exhibit and films on money and activities of the U.S. Treasury. Open Monday through Friday 9:30 A.M.–3:30 P.M. Closed holidays. Free. Time: 15–20 minutes.

Continue along Madison Place, Lafayette Square; cross Pennsylvania Avenue to the left of the White House. Facing you is the magnificent **Treasury Building (10)**, which houses the offices of the Secretary of the Treasury and provides for the sale of bonds and securities. Built between 1836 and 1869, and designed successively by Robert Mills, Thomas Ustick Walter, Ammi B. Young, Isaiah Rogers, and Mullett, it is an outstanding example of the Greek Revival style.

The Treasury Building was erected in four stages. The east side and central wing were built between 1836 and 1842 and designed by Mills. Compelled by Congress to economize, he had to use sandstone from government quarries, rather than the granite he preferred for the exterior. Yet the result is a large, fireproof building of dramatic design. Mills adopted the Greek Revival style then in vogue, and on the 15th Street facade devised a monumental Ionic colonnade 342 feet in length and three stories high. Walter's contribution, on the other hand, appears not to have extended beyond a small-scale plan that set out the general scheme for enlarging the building.

Although I made it the subject of my illustration, the south wing built between 1855 and 1861 by Young, is less impressive than the rest of the building. Not only is the structure different, but it is also built entirely in granite. A redeeming feature is James Earle Fraser's fine statue (1923) of Alexander Hamilton (1757–1804), the first Secretary of the Treasury, who died the victim of a duel with Aaron Burr. Daniel Webster's famous tribute to Hamilton's ability as Secretary of the Treasury is inscribed on the pedestal: "He smote the rock of the national resources and abundant streams of revenue gushed forth. He touched the dead corpse of the public credit and it sprang upon its feet."

The west wing, by Rogers, built between 1867 and 1869, completed this vast building. The interiors (open to the public by special permit only) of

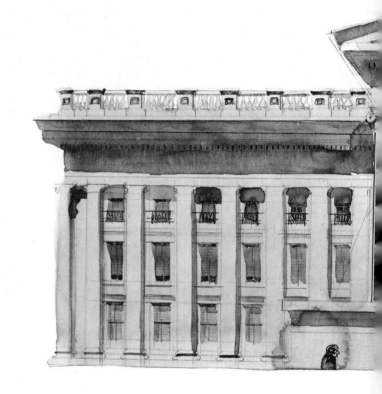

Treasury Building

these three wings of the Treasury Building are more richly decorated than the Mills portion. Young, Rogers, and especially Mullett made imaginative use of cast-plaster and cast-iron decoration. In the Cash Room of the north wing, Mullett created the most extraordinary room in the entire building, using seven varieties of marble to face the walls, embellished by bronze balcony railings.

The north wing, or front, makes a dramatic setting for another excellent statue (1947, Fraser), that of Swiss-born Albert Gallatin (1761–1849), Secretary of the Treasury during the Jefferson administration (1801–1809). He favored light taxes but the War of 1812 thwarted his attempts to bring about lasting financial stability.

The Treasury Building

Continue south along 15th Street until you come to one of Washington's most famous pub restaurants, **Old Ebbitt Grill***.

Old Ebbitt Grill

675 15th Street, NW. Telephone: (202)347-4801. Reservations accepted. Lunch 11:00 A.M.–2:00 P.M. Dinner 5:00 P.M.–12:00 MIDNIGHT; sandwiches served until 1:00 A.M.

The history of the grill, once part of Ebbitt's Hotel on 14th and E Street, NW, goes back to 1856. The hotel was demolished in 1926, and the grill, which was located at 14th and F Streets, was razed in 1983. Much of the old woodwork and fixtures, which came from Old Ebbitt's Dutch Room, and the side paneling once part of the English Room, were saved and installed in the new bar. The Old Ebbitt Bear once decorated the private bar of Alexander Hamilton. Long patronized by Presidents in and out of office, from Grant to Harding, and countless more hard-drinking politicos and correspondents, Old Ebbitt remains a perennial favorite with a lively mix of Washingtonians and visitors. The 'new' Old Ebbitt despite its Americana is no longer a National Historic Landmark. Nonetheless it is a pleasant place to have lunch.

A few more steps bring us to Pennsylvania Avenue and the magnificent vista stretching to the Capitol.

This part of Pennsylvania Avenue, or as it is sometimes called, "The Avenue," was planned by L'Enfant and is 1.2 miles long. A National Historic Site since 1965, it includes many of the most important elements of L'Enfant's plan for the Federal City, joining the White House to the Capitol and such historically related areas as the Federal Triangle, Judiciary Square, the National Portrait Gallery (the former Patent Office), and much of downtown Washington's older business district.

Since the middle of the nineteenth century, Pennsylvania Avenue has been the nation's principal ceremonial way, the site of countless inaugural parades, victory parades, funeral processions, and other public ceremonies of great national importance. Perhaps the most moving of these were the two events that followed the end of the Civil War. On April 19, 1865, thirty thousand people followed Lincoln's black-velvet-draped catafalque drawn by six cavalry horses as it moved down the Avenue from the White House to the Capitol. Among the marchers were convalescent soldiers, many on crutches, and four thousand black citizens in high silk hats. The second took place on May 23, 1865, when the greatest victory parade in American history took place. Two hundred thousand men of the Grand Army of the Republic marched past a reviewing stand in front of the White House. In more recent times, John F. Kennedy's funeral procession moved down the historic avenue, watched by millions on television throughout the world, as well as tens of thousands on the spot.

Proceed down Pennsylvania Avenue to 14th Street, to view the undistinguished statue of a grimly determined **Alexander Robey Shepherd*** (1835–1903) by U.S.J. Dunbar (1909). A controversial figure, he was the most influential force, next to L'Enfant, in shaping the Federal City. Boss Shepherd rammed through an $18 million program of civic improvement that made Washington look like a battlefield for over a decade. Between 1871 and 1889, the city was given for the first time an efficient drainage system, graded streets, and asphalt paving. The malarial Washington Canal was filled in, and the Capitol grounds were landscaped by Frederick Law Olmstead, Jr. (son of the designer of New York's Central Park).

Willard Hotel

Look now across the avenue at the **Willard Hotel (11)** on the corner of 14th Street. Closed and left derelict for more than a decade, it was once Washington's grandest, built in 1901 on the site of the Old Willard Hotel (1847–1901). There has been a hotel on this site since 1818 and in each, Tennison's Hotel, Williamson's Mansion Hotel, Fuller's American House, and the City Hotel, the register of distinguished guests was long.

Old Willard was the most historic. It was the scene of the ill-fated Washington Conference (February 4–27, 1861), the last major effort to save the Union. Throughout the Civil War, Old Willard burst at the seams with distinguished guests. "It is," wrote Nathaniel Hawthorne, "the meeting place of the true representatives of the country. You exchange nods with governors of sovereign states; elbow illustrious men, and tread on the toes of generals; you hear statesmen and orators speaking in familiar tones. You are mixed up with the office-seekers, wirepullers, inventors, artists, poets, editors, army correspondents, attachés of foreign lands and longwinded talkers, diplomatists, mail contractors, railway directors until your own identity is lost." Its guests included the Prince of Wales (Edward VII); Julia Ward Howe, who wrote the "Battle Hymn of the Republic" there; Charles Dickens; Henry Irving; Jenny Lind; Adelina Patti; and Buffalo Bill Cody.

Old Willard was demolished to make way for the present building designed by Henry Janeway Hardenbergh, the architect of the New York Plaza. It is an imposing example of the Beaux-Arts style. The clifflike twelve-story structure rises 130 feet to a parapet topped with an elaborate mansard roof and châteauesque turrets that are at the present time a giant refuge for wayward pigeons. Like its illustrious predecessor, the new hotel became the social and political center of Washington. Taft and Woodrow Wilson stayed here. Coolidge used the third floor as a temporary White House following the death of Harding. Other notable guests have included Lloyd George, John Philip Sousa, Albert Einstein, and Mark Twain, who wrote two books here in the early 1900s.

After World War II, Pennsylvania Avenue ceased to be the prime location of Washington's grand

Willard Hotel

hotels. The Willard gradually declined. Finally, the end came on July 15, 1968, when a notice was slapped under the door of each room at 3:00 P.M. informing the occupant that the hotel would be closed after midnight. Its days of glory ended, the famous old hotel was then stripped of its furnishings at an auction and threatened with demolition before being granted a reprieve as a National Historic Landmark. The plans of the Pennsylvania Avenue Development Corporation call for its reopening as a hotel in the summer of 1986. The Willard now under renovation awaits a new life, together with other historic buildings along The Avenue.

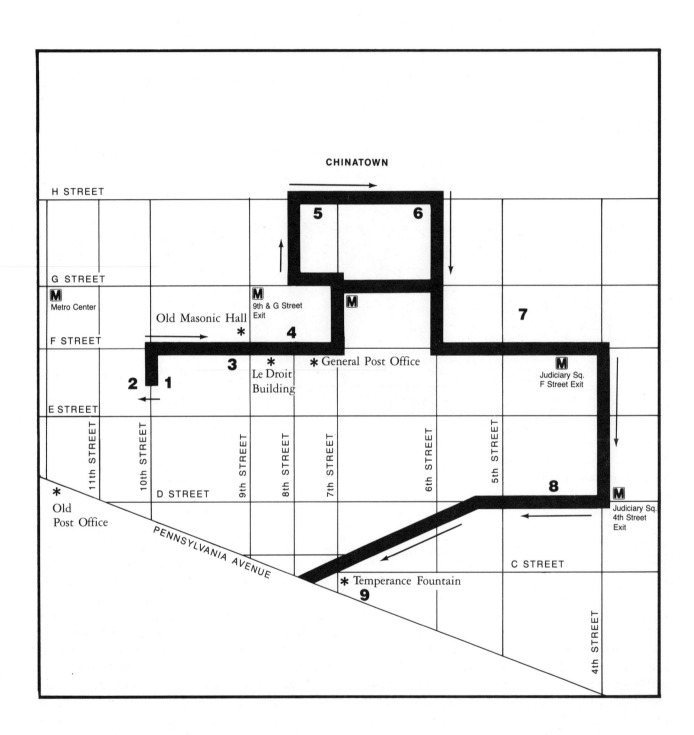

CHINATOWN

H STREET

5　　　　　6

G STREET

M Metro Center

M 9th & G Street Exit

Old Masonic Hall

M

F STREET

4

3

Le Droit Building

* General Post Office

7

M Judiciary Sq. F Street Exit

2　1

E STREET

* Old Post Office

11th STREET

10th STREET

D STREET

9th STREET

8th STREET

7th STREET

6th STREET

5th STREET

8

M Judiciary Sq. 4th Street Exit

PENNSYLVANIA AVENUE

C STREET

* Temperance Fountain

9

4th STREET

Downtown

Distance: 2 miles. Time: 3 hours. Metro: Metro Center (11th and G) or Federal Triangle (12th between Pennsylvania and Constitution). Metrobus: from Georgetown (M Street) take eastbound 30, 32, 34, 36, and M6 (to Pennsylvania and 10th); from Connecticut Avenue take southbound 42 (to 10th and F). Parking: commercial lots along Pennsylvania Avenue and F Street. Restaurants: Old Post Office; National Museum of American Art; Chinese restaurants on H Street between 6th and 8th Streets, NW; light food establishments on F between 8th and 10th.

Downtown was for many decades official Washington. The majority of the government buildings were concentrated between the Capitol and the White House and north of Pennsylvania Avenue. The Old Patent Office, Old City Hall (now Superior Court of the District of Columbia), and the Old Post Office were all within walking distance for the people who worked there. Secretaries of State, Senators, and Congressmen resided in mansions, hotels, and boarding houses along E, F, and G Streets.

Downtown was also Washington's business district. After the Civil War Pennsylvania Avenue, previously the city's primary commercial artery, declined in importance, while F Street boomed as the location for a new and more desirable business district. After 1870 many schools and churches were also built to accommodate the rapidly growing population.

Though much has changed, the downtown area remains one of the most interesting to explore, especially for Civil War buffs and lovers of Victorian architecture. Here you can visit several locations associated with those stormy years between 1861 and 1865: the scenes of Lincoln's inaugural balls, the Surratt House where much of the conspiracy to assassinate Lincoln was planned, Ford's Theatre where Lincoln was assassinated, and the Petersen House where Lincoln died. Last, but certainly not least, the location of the studio of the pioneer photographer Mathew Brady.

Downtown also includes many Victorian houses, department stores, and public buildings, a goodly number of which are being restored by the Pennsylvania Avenue Development Corporation. An engaging mini-Chinatown is located here too, full of colorful shops and good inexpensive restaurants. The Chinese New Year's parade, as elsewhere, attracts many thousands to H Street each year.

If you only have a limited amount of time, but wish to visit the historically significant places, you might wish to restrict yourself to visiting those buildings associated with Lincoln's last hours— Ford's Theatre, the Petersen House, Booth's Escape Route, and the Surratt House. The hour or so you will spend doing so will be one of the most memorable in your entire visit to the Federal City.

Old Post Office

1100 Pennsylvania Avenue, NW. Telephone: (202)289-4224. Boutiques, resturants and Federal offices. Observation deck located in clock tower.

We begin our tour of the downtown area at the Old Post Office. Once considered an unsightly blight, the **Old Post Office*** now stands as a shining example of "American architecture" and adaptive re-use. Called a "cross between a cathedral and a cotton mill" by *The New York Times* in 1899, the Romanesque wedding cake of Maine granite has been the subject of much criticism and controversy.

Completed in 1899, the Old Post Office was designed in 1892 by Willoughby J. Edbrooke, supervisory architect for the Treasury, and is the capital's oldest Federal building. (It was here that the postal employees successfully campaigned for the first Flag Day, June 14, 1908.) The building's design is reminiscent of the work of architect H. H. Richardson, who used the rough stonework and massive arches inspired by twelfth-century Romanesque architecture of southern France, and was soon out of date shortly after its completion. The trend toward classicism, embodied by the Beaux-Art style which was introduced in the United States in 1893, soon led to the call for the destruction of the Old Post Office because it would detract from the neoclassic architecture that was to characterize the Federal Triangle. The Depression halted a scheme to raze the building in 1934, and the "Old Tooth," as it was known, became home to various government agencies, including the FBI. The Old Post Office received another reprieve from the wrecker's ball in 1971 when a group of preservationists rallied and put an end to its uncertain fate. Twelve years later the "renewed" Old Post Office was reopened to public acclaim.

Little has changed. The architects in charge of the restoration—Arthur Cotton Moore, Assoc., of Washington, D.C. envisioned the building as a bridge between the local city to the north and the Federal enclave to the south and sought to retain the building's intricate carvings, marble pillars, elaborate arches, deeply relieved walls, pointed dormers, and 315-foot clock tower.

Central to the project was the restoration of an impressive atrium, which rises 196 feet to a glass roof. Seven floors of office space and three floors of commercial retail space overlook this vast interior court and a stage that provides entertainment seven days and six evenings a week. Ten bells, replicas of those in Westminster Abbey (and cast in the same foundry) ring from the clock tower. The bells were a Bicentennial gift to the United States from the Ditchley Foundation of Great Britain. A glass-enclosed elevator lifts visitors to an observation deck where a panoramic view of the city unfolds from the second highest pinnacle in the area. A favorite spot for watching parades during McKinley's inauguration, the Old Post Office with its marble balustrades, brass railings, refinished red oak woodwork, and creamy pink and gray marble today provides a welcome respite from the neighboring government buildings.

Proceed east on Pennsylvania Avenue one block to 10th Street and then walk north on 10th. Ford's Theatre National Historic Site is located between E and F Streets on 10th.

Ford's Theatre National Historic Site

511 10th Street, NW. Ford's Theatre National Historic Site, including the Petersen House, is administered by the National Park Service. Telephone: (202)426-6924. Open daily 9:00 A.M.–5:00 P.M. Closed Christmas. Free. Historical talks every hour on the half-hour from 9:30 A.M.–4:30 P.M. Time: allow 1 hour for the whole complex.

On the night of April 14, 1865, President Abraham Lincoln went to see the last performance of the two-week run of *Our American Cousin* at **Ford's Theatre (1)**. The Lincolns were accompanied by a military aide, Major Henry Rathbone, and his fianceé, Clara Harris. John Parker, a bodyguard, was stationed outside the State Box but later left his post to watch the play from the dress circle.

Our American Cousin was written by Tom Taylor, an Englishman who was the most popular dramatist on both sides of the Atlantic at the time. The play was a farce about members of an English upper-class family who, upon settling an estate, discover an American cousin who is entitled to his share. Asa Trenchard, the Yankee cousin played by Harry Hawk, is invited to England so that he can be cheated out of his inheritance. But the wily American beats them at their own game.

The play was already drawing the applause of a crowded house as the Presidential party was seated. Stage action stopped for a few minutes as the orchestra struck up "Hail to the Chief." A haggard Lincoln bowed in response and the play resumed. The formidable Mrs. Mountchessington (Mrs. H. Muzzy), who has been trying to marry off her daughter Augusta to Asa on the assumption he is rich, discovers he is not. She tells him that he is not used to the manners of good society and flounces offstage leaving the hero to put his thumbs in his waistcoat and call her "a sockdologizing old man trap!" As the audience laughed, comedy gave way to tragedy. Actor John Wilkes Booth, a twenty-six-year-old Confederate sympathizer, climbed the winding stairs to the State Box, turned the knob and slowly pushed open the unlocked, unguarded door.

The next scene was one of shock, confusion, and terror as Booth fired at the back of the President's head. Hearing the shot, Rathbone turned and grappled with the assassin, but Booth slashed him across

Ford's Theatre National Historic Site

the arm with a hunting knife. Jumping to the stage, Booth caught his spur in one of the flags draping the box and fell heavily, breaking his left leg. The audience, stupiefied, watched the actor cross the stage at a limping run; in the State Box, Mrs. Lincoln gave a piercing scream as Booth escaped through the wings. The dying Lincoln was carried across the street to the home of William Petersen. There at 7:22 the following morning, Abraham Lincoln, fifty-six, the sixteenth President of the United States, died.

Ford's Theatre quickly became the target of anxiety. Cries of "Burn the theater" went up as the news of the assassination spread, and the building, one of Washington's most popular playhouses, was closed

by the War Department. Its owner, John Ford, was arrested and held for thirty-nine days before he was cleared of any involvement in the conspiracy. He planned to reopen the theater in June 1865, but the proposal aroused so much public indignation that it was closed a second time. Eventually the building was acquired by the War Department to house the office of records and pensions of Union veterans and the Army Medical Museum. Later, the building served as a publications depot for the Adjutant General. It was not until February 13, 1968, that Ford's Theatre opened its doors to the public once more.

Today, the historic theater has been restored to look exactly as it did in 1865. The State Box is decorated and furnished as it was on the night of the assassination. President Lincoln occupied the rocking chair; Mrs. Lincoln sat in a straight, cane-bottomed chair at his right; Major Rathbone was on the sofa; and Clara Harris was seated in the upholstered chair. The crimson damask sofa is original but the other pieces were duplicated for the restoration. The flags displayed across the front of the box are also reproductions, but the gilt-framed steel engraving of George Washington was actually there on the fateful night.

The stage is set for the second scene of the third act of *Our American Cousin*, the point in the performance when Lincoln was shot. Booth, who knew every line, planned his move when only Harry Hawk was onstage and the audience laughing at his exit line. When the time came, Booth entered the box to shoot Lincoln. You can trace the rest of his movements through the dress circle and view the State Box.

In the basement, the **Lincoln Museum** illustrates Lincoln's life as frontier lawyer, philosopher, and statesman, with a motley collection of artifacts and memorabilia from every period of his life. Here is the Treasury flag on which Booth caught his spur, and the long black boot worn by the actor with the slit made by Dr. Samuel Mudd to treat his injured leg. Also on view is the small brass single-shot, muzzle-loading derringer pistol from which the fatal bullet was fired.

As you come out of the theater glance at the box office next door. This is a reconstruction of the **Star Tavern** where Booth took a slug of whiskey before entering the theater to carry out his plan. If you are wondering what happened to the original front door of this celebrated bar, you might be interested to learn that it's in Georgetown still serving as a front door to a private home.

Petersen House

Across the street from Ford's Theatre (516 10th Street, NW) is the **Petersen House (2)**, also known as the "House Where Lincoln Died," which was built in 1849.

Petersen House (House Where Lincoln Died)

As the stricken President was carried from the theater, a man with a candle appeared on the front steps of this red-brick rowhouse. It was Petersen, a tailor. Dr. Charles Leale, twenty-three-year-old assistant surgeon, United States Volunteers, decided to have Lincoln carried into the house and followed Petersen to a quiet back bedroom on the first floor. While Leale was doing what he could to comfort the dying President, the parlor next to the bedroom became a bustling seat of government presided over by Secretary of War Stanton. As the anguished Mary

Todd Lincoln wept in the front parlor, comforted by her eldest son, Robert, and actress Laura Keene, the imperious Stanton began investigating the assassination and administered the oath of succession to Vice-President Andrew Johnson.

Only part of the house is open to the public. The three historic rooms are furnished with replicas or furnishings of the same period and design. The total effect seems like a rerun of the tragedy in a house strangely haunted. The small back bedroom where Lincoln died contributes especially to this mood: the Victorian wallpaper, a simple washstand with a cracked white bowl. On the walls are framed prints of *The Village Blacksmith* and Rosa Bonheur's *Horse Fair*; still standing is the simple bed that was too small for the unfortunate President.

Continue up 10th to F Street. Turn right on F and walk to view **Booth's Escape Route (3)**, an alley between 10th and 9th Streets, with an exit between 918 and 920 F Street. Though the area bears little resemblance to its appearance in 1865, it nonetheless looks strangely sordid. "Association does," to quote Henry James, " simply what it likes with us." After he shot Lincoln, Booth made his way to the back door of the theater where he had left his horse. Seizing the reins from doorman Johnny Peanut Burroughs, he spurred his horse and galloped through the alley to 9th Street, then right to Pennsylvania Avenue and rode toward the Capitol, down to the Navy Yard into Maryland, and then back into Virginia, where he was shot to death at the Garrett farm some twelve days later. [Visitors who would like to tour the entire 225-mile escape route can find a tour through the Surratt Society, the Smithsonian, or Marker Tours. The tours are usually offered in spring and fall.]

Today, this part of F Street contains some interesting Victorian public buildings. Among them is the once-magnificent **Old Masonic Hall***, at the northwest corner of 9th and F Streets. The building, designed in French Renaissance style by Adolph Cluss and Joseph Wildrich von Kammerrheuber, was built between 1868 and 1870. At the time of its construction, the neighborhood was highly fashionable, with fine mansions as well as government buildings such as the Post Office and the Old Patent Office. The cornerstone was laid in May 1868, amid great public ceremony. Led by President Andrew Johnson, a Master Mason, the Masons of Washington marched in a procession from the corner of 9th and D Streets, NW, down Pennsylvania Avenue

Booth's Escape Route

past the Treasury Building to their new temple.

By 1876 the Old Masonic Hall was the scene of the capital's most brilliant balls and state occasions. Some of the more notable included a banquet given by the British Minister for the Prince of Wales, and a mass debutantes' party given by silver magnate Senator William Stewart, at which, according to one account, "So, such nakedness was probably never before revealed in Washington."

By the 1890s, however, the building was not grand or big enough, and in 1908 the Masons moved to their present headquarters at 13th Street and New York Avenue. The old hall began a slow slide to decline, reaching rock bottom in 1921 when it was leased and subsequently sold to the Lansburgh Company. Most of the cast-iron and ornaments were removed or painted over as was the facade, thus obliterating much of its original character. Now vacant, the hall has been the subject of some interest and one day may be restored to its former beauty.

Cross 9th and continue on F to the **Le Droit Building***, on the southwest corner of 8th and F Streets. Built in 1875 and designed by James H. McGill in the Italian Revival style of the period, the Le Droit Building was intended exclusively for use as offices. Today, the large north-facing windows have made it a favorite studio block for many of Washington's artists.

At the southeast corner of 8th and F Streets, is a classical **Post Office***, formerly the General Post Office and now shared by the F Street station post office and the Federal Trade Commission. A National Historic Landmark it is not open to the public. Designed by Robert Mills in 1839 and built on a site occupied by Samuel Blodgett's hotel, which the government purchased to house a temporary post office and patent office, this graceful building is one of the oldest of the great public edifices of the Federal City. Dickens thought it "a very compact and very beautiful building." After Mills's death, a northern wing along F Street, designed by Thomas Ustick Walter (1804–1887), was begun in 1855 but not completed until after the Civil War, in 1866.

The Charleston-born Robert Mills (1781–1855) was among the first Americans to achieve recognition as an architect. After being articled to Latrobe (1803–08) in Philadelphia, he practiced in the Quaker City before coming to Washington where he worked with Hoban and again, Latrobe. Jefferson gave him encouragement and allowed him the privilege of using his famous architectural library. At this point, however, Mills returned to Charleston as state engineer and town architect, designing many distinctive and superb buildings there. But President Andrew Jackson summoned him back in 1836, appointing him architect of public buildings in Washington. In this post he designed and supervised the construction of the Treasury Building (see page 26) and the Patent Office and Post Office; he also designed the Washington Monument, which was built without the base he originally planned.

Turn now to view the Old Patent Office.

Old Patent Office

Between 7th and 9th and F and G Streets, NW. A National Historic Landmark owned by the Smithsonian Institution. Houses the National Portrait Gallery (entrance on F Street) and the National Museum of American Art (entrance on G Street). Telephone: (202)357-2700 for general tourist information. Metro stop: Gallery Place (7th and G). Open daily 10:00 A.M.–5:30 P.M. Closed Christmas. Free. Walk-in tours available at 12:00 NOON on weekdays and 1:45 P.M. on Sundays. To make reservations for group tours call (202)357-3111. Entrance for the handicapped through parking ramp on G Street. Time: 1 hour, add another hour if you plan to see both museums.

Begun in 1836 and completed in 1867, the **Old Patent Office** (4) symbolizes the importance that the youthful United States attached to invention. The Doric portico, a replica of the Parthenon, towers above the F Street plaza like a Temple of Power

Old Patent Office (National Portrait Gallery and National Museum of American Art)

through Knowledge, which in fact it is. Designed by William P. Elliott, with additions by Robert Mills, Thomas U. Walter, and Edward Clark, the monumental building ranks with the White House, the Capitol, and the Treasury as one of the great examples of Greek Revival architecture in America.

During the Civil War, it also served as barracks hospital and morgue. The First Rhode Island Militia was billeted in bunks throughout the building, and after the bloody battles of Second Bull Run,

Antietam, and Fredericksburg, 2,000 beds were placed on the marble floors to cope with the wounded. Walt Whitman, a clerk in the building employed by the Bureau of Indian Affairs, was a volunteer nurse also, and in 1863 wrote, "I go at night to soothe and relieve particular cases." His "Wound-Dresser" was one of the poems inspired by what he saw there.

In March 1865, Lincoln's second inaugural ball was held in the gas-lit building; 4,000 guests went through the receiving line in a third-floor gallery (now known as the Lincoln Gallery) before dancing to waltzes and polkas. Whitman paid another visit on this occasion. "What a different scene they [the galleries] presented to my view a while since, filled with a crowded mass of the worst wounded of the war."

The Patent Office resumed recording inventions and issuing patents. Some idea of the magnitude of the task may be gathered from the fact that between 1836 and 1892 about five hundred thousand patents were granted in the United States as compared to the one hundred fifty thousand issued in Britain since 1621. Inventors flocked to Washington to consult the Patent Office scientific library with its invaluable duplicate records of comparable British and German inventions, as well as to lobby for financial backing and favorable legislation. They included Alexander Graham Bell, the inventor of the telephone; Thomas Edison, inventor of the incandescent light bulb and other electrical devices; and Cyrus McCormick, inventor of the reaping machine. Their inventions, among many others, led to the harvesting of America's incredibly rich natural resources, which in turn would create unprecedented wealth through industrial expansion.

Until the disastrous fire of September 1877 completely devastated the Model Halls, the Model Museum on the second floor also made the Patent Office a mecca for the Victorian visitor and one of the great showplaces of the capital. Nearly one hundred thousand accepted patent models went up in flames. The Declaration of Independence was saved, however, and the building was restored to its original exterior design. The remarkable Victorian third floor, with its cast-iron staircases, colored etched-glass window doors with medallions of great inventors (designed by Cluss and Von Ezdorf) date from this time.

The Department of the Interior vacated the building in 1917. The Patent Office remained until 1932 when the Civil Service Commission took it over until 1963. For a year or so after that, it seemed likely that the great old building would be demolished to make way for the inevitable parking lot. Fortunately, a dramatic appeal to President Eisenhower succeeded in transferring the building to the Smithsonian Institution in 1958 for use as public art galleries.

Established by Congress in 1962, the **National Portrait Gallery** opened to the public in 1968. Its collection focuses on portraits of the persons who have changed or enriched the course of history and development of the United States. Special thematic exhibits, mainly of portraits borrowed from outside sources, supplement the gallery's permanent collections.

The **National Museum of American Art**, on the other hand, is a museum devoted to American art. Although the collection has been in existence for well over a century, it was virtually inaccessible to the general public until housed here. Outstanding parts of this huge collection (over thirty thousand paintings, sculptures, prints, photographs, and drawings) include the celebrated Indian paintings by George Catlin (1796–1872), works from the New Deal's Federal Art Project, and an ongoing collection of modern art.

Both museums excel in in-depth presentations of the American experience that make exhibition-going an unexpected delight. If you have the time, do make the effort to see whatever is being shown.

Now walk to the corner of 8th and H Streets to view Calvary Baptist Church.

Calvary Baptist Church

755 8th Street, NW. Telephone: Monday through Friday (202)347-8355. Open daily (entrance through Woodward Building). Services: Sunday 10:15 A.M. (deaf worship) and 10:45 A.M. Visitors welcome. Time: 15 minutes.

Calvary Baptist Church (5) was built between 1864 and 1866 in stylish Victorian red brick by Adolph Cluss, who later designed the Arts and Industries Building of the Smithsonian Institution. Destroyed by fire in 1867, it was rebuilt in 1869 and has long been famous as one of the most progressive churches of the city.

The congregation itself was organized during the

Calvary Baptist Church

Civil War by pro-Union and antislavery Northern Baptists. One of its early leading spirits was Amos Kendall, Jackson's Postmaster-General and chief figure in the so-called "kitchen cabinet," whose deeply motivated concern for deaf children made him one of the most unusual philanthropists in an age of philanthropy. Kendall took poor children into his own house and began teaching them to read and write while he and his friends pressured Congress to appropriate funds to establish the Columbia Institution for the Deaf, Dumb and Blind. He deeded his land and even his country house to this institution and placed Dr. Edward Gallaudet, a qualified teacher, in charge. Gallaudet (after whom the Gallaudet College for the Deaf was named) founded the first Washington mission for deaf mutes at Calvary Baptist in 1885, and it continues today.

In 1894 James G. Hill designed Woodward Building, the Sunday School building named for S. Walter Woodward (of Woodward & Lothrop), who held such strong religious convictions that he stopped the sale of playing cards and dice in his store and gave away thousands in the true Boston Brahmin tradition.

The interior has much of the simplicity of colonial churches laced with engagingly Victorian trimmings and accents. Notice also the giant Mohler organ with its five thousand pipes, installed in 1927.

Continue along H Street at an easy pace and pretend that the Civil War has just ended. At 604 H Street is the Surratt House where Booth and fellow conspirators met to plan the assassination of Lincoln.

39

Surratt House

Surratt House

604 H Street, NW. A National Historic Landmark. Not open to the public.

Located in the bustling heart of Washington's Chinatown, the Federal-style **Surratt House (6)** is a constant reminder of the Lincoln assassination. So much so, that when I was at work drawing it, a parking-lot attendant glanced over my shoulder and asked if I knew "anything about the house?" adding that, "After what happened there, they should have torn the place down!" Yet time itself has touched the old house lightly, although some alterations were made in 1921 to accommodate a shop at street level (now a Chinese grocery store).

Surratt House derives its historical significance from its intimate connection with the plot to abduct Lincoln, which later developed into his assassination. Mary Surratt, a forty-five-year-old Maryland widow, rented the building from 1864 to 1865 and used it as a boardinghouse. Here, Lewis Powell (alias Paine) and George Atzerodt, two of the conspirators who were boarders, and John Wilkes Booth, a frequent visitor, discussed their plans with Mary Surratt's errant son, John, and several other boarders. Originally, the conspirators planned to kidnap Lincoln, Vice-President Johnson, General Grant, and members of the cabinet. But when the Confederacy collapsed, Booth decided on assassination. As we know, he was successful in carrying out his part of the plot, though Paine failed in his attempt to kill Secretary of State Seward at his home on Lafayette Square.

Mary Surratt was jailed in the Old Brick Capitol for allegedly having taken part in the plot. Along with Paine, Atzerodt, and Davy Herold, she was tried by a military court in the Arsenal Penitentiary (Fort McNair) and found guilty. Only later, when the testimony of witnesses was sifted and the court records carefully reexamined was it obvious that she was innocent. A Supreme Court ruling later declared such military tribunals unconstitutional. The unfortunate Mary, who was a Roman Catholic, was not even allowed to see a priest before or during the trial. When she was finally allowed to see Father Walter on the day before her execution, he had to promise to say nothing of her innocence in order to get the necessary pass from Stanton. She spent her last hours weeping before being fitted with a hood and hanged in the courtyard of the penitentiary on July 7, 1865.

Within a few years after her death, there were reports of something strange going on at the old boardinghouse. The property changed hands so often that it attracted the attention of contemporary journalists, who set down the tales former owners had told them. Most dealt with ominous sounds and muffled whispers thought to be the conspirators going over their plans. But the creaking of boards on the second floor was caused by Mary herself, doomed for all eternity to walk Washington until her name was cleared.

Proceed now to Metro Station Gallery Place at the corner of 7th and G Streets and take the train to Judiciary Square. Or, walk down 6th to F Street, turn left on F to 5th Street to your next stop, the Old Pension Building.

Old Pension Building

North Judiciary Square at 5th and G Streets, NW. A National Historic Landmark owned by the Federal government, the Pension Building is the home of the National Building Museum. Telephone: (202)272-2448. Open Monday through Friday 10:00 A.M.–5:00 P.M. Closed federal holidays. In addition to exhibits, there are regularly scheduled tours of the building itself; call for times and reservations.

If you caught Metro's Red Line to Judiciary Square, you are in for a visual surprise. The F Street escalator shoots you up to one of the most spectacular Victorian buildings in the United States, the **Old Pension Building** (7). Built between 1882 and 1887, after the passage of the Arrears Act in 1879 that greatly expanded the scope of the federal pension program, the building was designed by army engineer Major General Montgomery C. Meigs, former Quartermaster-General of the Union Army.

On the exterior the vast rectangular building with its row upon row of pedimented windows resembles the sixteenth-century Palazzo Farnese, which had caught Meigs's eye during an 1867 visit to Italy. Notice the 3-foot-high terra-cotta frieze (Casper Buberl, 1834–1889) that extends 1,200 feet around the exterior of the entire building and depicts military forces on the march. Allegorical figures representing Peace and War grace the spandrels of the four entrance arches or gates; respectively named the Gate of the Invalids (north), Gate of the Quartermaster (west), Gate of the Infantry (south), and Gate of the Navy (east).

Built of 15 million bricks, the Pension Building consists of a series of interconnecting rooms—each entered from an arcaded loggia—arranged around an open central space. Meigs, concerned with the health of the office workers, wanted a building that would have natural light and fresh air in every office space. He designed one in which fresh air entered by means of passageways underneath each window, flowed through the offices out into the soaring space of the Great Hall and then up and out through windows high above.

Old Pension Building (National Building Museum)

This vast courtyard (316 feet by 116 feet) with its 75-foot-high Corinthian columns made the Pension Building a favorite venue for the enormous inaugurals of Presidents Cleveland, Harrison, McKinley, Theodore Roosevelt, Taft, Nixon, Carter, and Reagan. Newly renovated, it continues to be one of the sites of the Presidential Inaugural Ball.

After the Pension Bureau was moved out in 1926, the Pension Building was used by many government agencies. In 1980 Congress passed legislation making it the home of the National Building Museum, a nonprofit organization whose purpose is to commemorate and encourage the American building arts.

Old City Hall

451 Indiana Avenue, NW. A National Historic Landmark owned by the Federal government. Houses the Superior Court of the District of Columbia. Open Monday through Friday 9:00 A.M.–4:00 P.M. Closed holidays. Time: 15 minutes. No guided tour.

Leaving the Old Pension Building, resume your walk along F to 4th Street. Now turn right to Indiana Avenue. One block up is the historic **Old City Hall (8)**, the first public building constructed to house the District of Columbia government. Built in 1820, this handsome edifice with its Ionic portico, has served as city hall, slavemarket, courthouse, Civil War hospital, and Federal offices. In-

Old City Hall (Superior Court of the District of Columbia)

side, you will admire the main hall, embellished with marble floors, pilasters, and columns. Double staircases leading to the second floor have marble steps and elegant cast-iron handrails.

As a courthouse, Old City Hall was the scene of many famous trials. The final act of the Lincoln conspiracy was enacted here in 1867 when John Surratt, who had fled to Canada after the assassination, was caught and tried. He denied taking part in Lincoln's murder, but admitted being involved in the plot to kidnap the President. The jury could not agree on a verdict and he was acquitted. Charles Guiteau, President Garfield's assassin, was also tried here, as were Secretary of the Interior Albert Fall and oil operator Harry Sinclair, both of whom were involved in the Teapot Dome scandals during the Harding administration.

Old City Hall, a superb example of Greek Revival, was designed by George Hadfield (*c.* 1764–1826), a talented English architect who came to the United States in 1795 in response to an invitation by the commissioners of the Federal City to act as superintendent of the Capitol, then under construction. Unfortunately, Hadfield's career in America was one of unfulfilled promise. He had been a prize student at the Royal Academy architectural school and had worked with James Wyatt in Rome. But he ran afoul of William Thornton, who designed the Capitol, and was not as resilient as Latrobe in handling that difficult dilettante. His most important building, the Treasury and Executive Office, was burned by the British in 1814. Old City Hall and Arlington House, however, survive as inspiring examples of his fine and graceful touch.

The Apex Building

633 Pennsylvania Avenue, NW. A National Historic Landmark.

From Old City Hall continue west on Indiana Avenue to 7th Street. Take a left on 7th and cross C Street. Stop at the **Temperance Fountain*** (*c.* 1880, Henry Cogswell) at 7th and Pennsylvania Avenue, a delightful Victorian minimonument presented by Connecticut Yankee Dr. Henry Cogswell, dentist and temperance crusader of San Francisco. Cogswell made a fortune from real estate and mining investments, and was one of the pioneers of false teeth. He donated fountains to whatever cities would accept them.

The **Apex Building (9)**, an unusual twin-towered brownstone structure built in 1859 (architect unknown) and remodeled in 1886 by Mullett for the Central National Bank, and a pair of mid-Victorian buildings that housed Mathew Brady's celebrated Washington studio now house the Sears World Trade Building. Best remembered for his great photographic chronicle of the Civil War, Mathew Brady (1823–1896) operated two galleries in New York and one in Washington. He specialized in depicting the notables of the day and it was here that he exhibited his "original portraits of distinguished persons." With the outbreak of the Civil War, Brady anticipated a big demand for photographs, and he organized and directed a corps of cameramen (poor eyesight prevented his own use of the camera) to record the conflict. But popular interest in his pictures did not materialize and the coming peace saw him bankrupt.

At this point Pennsylvania Avenue is a convenient place to conclude the Downtown tour. It is close to the parking lots of F Street and Metrobus connections. Metro stations Gallery Place, Archives, and Judiciary Square are also close by.

The Apex Building

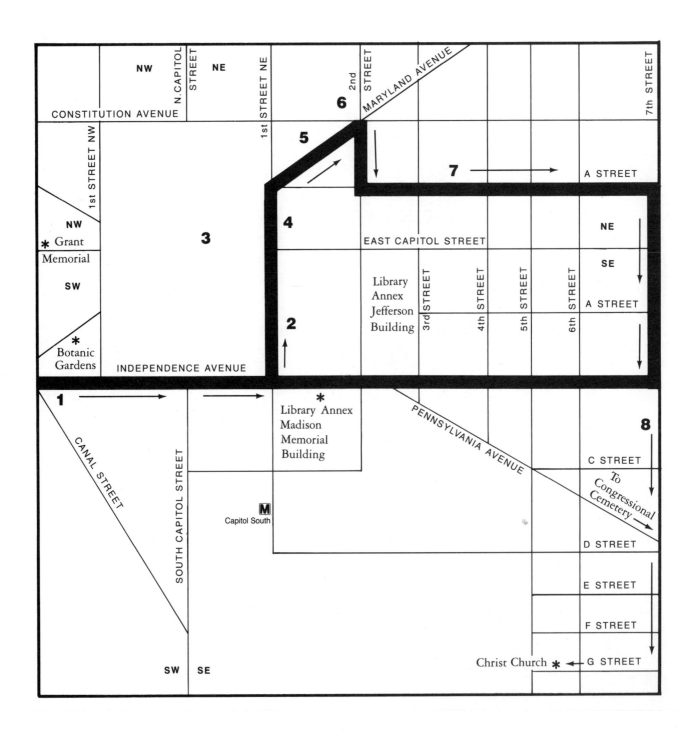

Capitol Hill

Distance: 2 miles. Time: 3 to 4 hours, depending on how long you spend in the U.S. Capitol. Metro: Federal Center (3rd and D). Metrobus: eastbound 30, 32, 34, and 36 along Pennsylvania Avenue (1st Street); westbound 40 along East Capitol Street (Capitol). Meter parking strictly limited. Use Smithsonian visitor parking garage under Air and Space Museum on 7th between Independence Avenue and Jefferson Drive, SW. Restaurants: in museums along Mall; National Gallery of Art has an excellent inexpensive restaurant and cafeteria; snack counters and cafeterias also at the Air and Space Museum, the Supreme Court, and the Library of Congress.

Capitol Hill takes its name from the hill that rises in the center of the city and extends westward. This hill, called Jenkins Hill and the site of Indian encampments when English settlers first ventured up the Potomac, was the site L'Enfant described as a "pedestal waiting for a monument." He placed the Capitol facing east because the southeast was the waterfront area, where he expected the main residential and business section to rise. Visitors would come up along East Capitol Street from the Potomac and thus see the front of the Capitol. But when railroads supplanted the port city, the main residential section emerged to the west and northwest as did the main business district.

For the Capitol building itself, Washington and Jefferson chose the design submitted by William Thornton. Progress was slow owing to labor shortages and the impracticality of Thornton's design. By 1800 only the Senate wing had been completed and it had to accommodate both houses of Congress, their library, *and* the Supreme Court. In 1814 the British burned the entire building, but under Latrobe's supervision, the Capitol was rebuilt.

The nation grew and so did the government, and quite beyond everyone's wildest dreams. Yet L'Enfant's avenues, squares, and parks superimposed on a standard grid of streets contained this breathless expansion. But more and more space was needed. During the Civil War, new wings were added to the Capitol, as well as a bigger dome. Following the war, the entire neighborhood boomed. Alexander "Boss" Shepherd's building program stimulated new construction; between 1870 and 1900, row upon row of townhouses—Eastlake, Second Empire, Richardsonian Romanesque, Queen Anne, and Jacobean, to name just a few styles—filled in the open spaces in the subdivided lots. The approaches to the Capitol itself, long littered with huge mounds of debris, were gradually transformed into a magnificent park.

Toward the turn of the century, further changes took place. The Library of Congress, bursting at the seams (it still is), got its splendidly ornate Italian Renaissance style building. Office blocks and apartment houses for Congressmen and other officials replaced boardinghouses, hotels, and taverns. The handsome Union Station, designed by Daniel Burnham, was built to the north in 1908 and became the depot for all the city's railroads. Finally, in 1935, the Supreme Court occupied its own building.

This walk around the original Capitol Hill (Eastern Market, Christ Church, and Congressional Cemetery are optional for reasons of time and distance), with its magnificent public buildings and monuments, shows how remarkable a vision L'Enfant had. The public buildings and monuments coupled with the wide range of private buildings dating from flat-fronted Federal houses to the flamboyant towers of Victorian rowhouses, give the Hill a fascinating architectural character. Both elements form part of the Capitol Hill Historic District designated in 1976 by the National Park Service as a National Historic Landmark.

Bartholdi Fountain

48

Bartholdi Fountain

Independence Avenue and Canal Street, SW.

We begin our tour of Capitol Hill at the celebrated **Bartholdi Fountain** (1), named for Frédéric Auguste Bartholdi (1834–1902), the sculptor of the Statue of Liberty. The fountain, supported by a trio of lusty bronze maidens, provides a touch of *la belle époque* Paris to its surroundings. Erected here in 1932, it was originally shown at the Philadelphia Centennial exhibition of 1876 (an impressive selection of centennial exhibits can be seen at the Smithsonian's Arts and Industries Building on the Mall). The United States government purchased the fountain at the close of the exhibition and first erected it in 1878 on the grounds of the old Botanic Garden, which was located at the foot of The Capitol.

Behind the fountain on Independence Avenue are the **United States Botanic Gardens*** at 1st and 2nd Streets, and B Street and Maryland Avenue, SW. Telephone: (202)225-7099. Open daily 9:00 A.M.–5:00 P.M.; closed Thanksgiving, Christmas, and New Year's Day. Free. Group tours by appointment only.

The Botanic Gardens were built in 1902 and enlarged between 1931 and 1933 to replace the original pavilion built in 1850 to house the botanical booty brought to Washington by various expeditions. It contains a remarkable collection of plants, as well as a subtropical forest area.

As you emerge from the Botanic Gardens, cross Maryland Avenue and follow the Capitol Reflecting Pool to view the massive **Ulysses S. Grant Memorial*** (1922, Henry Mervin Shrady), which forms the central and largest group of monumental sculptures in front of the Capitol. Grant is flanked by the Garfield Memorial (1887, J. Q. Adams Ward) and the Peace Monument (1877, Franklin Simmons). Like the Botanic Gardens, the Grant Memorial was part of the McMillan Plan of 1902, which sought to consummate L'Enfant's grand design by making Washington a city of buildings within parks embellished with memorials and fountains.

One of the largest equestrian groups in the world, the Grant memorial was not completed until 1922. Shrady worked on it for fifteen years, only to die two weeks before the unveiling. The brooding figure of

Grant strongly evokes his obsessive zeal in pursuing victory at whatever the cost. Notice also the right-hand group "posed by" a cadet battery of horse artillery at West Point.

Cross over to the elliptical road and walk east through the Capitol grounds to our next stop, the Library of Congress. Designed by Frederick Law Olmstead, the grounds on the western side are full of huge luxuriant trees and shrubbery.

Library of Congress

1st Street between East Capitol Street and Independence Avenue, SE. Telephone: (202)287-6400 (information). Metro: Capitol South (5-minute walk). The Main Reading Room, the Thomas Jefferson Building Reading Room, and the principal reading rooms are open Monday through Friday 8:30 A.M. –9:30 P.M., Saturday 8:30 A.M.–5:00 P.M., and Sunday 1:00–5:00 P.M. Free guided tour, lasting 45 minutes, leaves from the ground floor outside the orientation theater on the hour Monday through Friday 9:00 A.M.–4:00 P.M. Group tours must be arranged four to six weeks in advance; call tour office (202)287-5458. Snack bar on ground floor and the basement cafeteria are open to the public.

Just beyond the courtyard of the Capitol on 1st Street is the opulent Thomas Jefferson Building of the **Library of Congress (2)**, with its incandescent light-sepia granite walls, red-marble trim, and low-domed rotunda topped with a lantern and the *Torch of Learning* (1893, Edward Pearce Casey). Designed by the Washington architects John L. Smithmeyer and Paul J. Pelz, the library was built between 1889 and 1897 by the U.S. Army Corps of Engineers, under the supervision of General Thomas Lincoln Casey. His son, a New York architect, Edward Pearce Casey, completed the job afer General Casey died in 1902.

The Library of Congress was established in 1800 at the time the Federal government was being transferred from Philadelphia to Washington. Maintenance of the library proved to be a difficult task. Congress appropriated $5,000 for the purchase of books, which were destroyed by fire when Admiral Cockburn burned the Capitol. This terrible act of vandalism was sparked when Cockburn, seating himself in the Speaker's chair of the House of Representatives, called a mock assembly of officers to approve a motion that "this harbor of Yankee democracy be burned." After affirmative response,

Library of Congress

Lunchtime Concert on the Neptune
Plaza, Library of Congress

51

teams of soldiers and sailors vied with one another to collect books and documents for kindling. The original collection was replaced by the purchase of Jefferson's library in 1815. Living at that time in retirement at Monticello, and deep in debt, Jefferson agonized over the destruction of the library. He sold the government some sixty-five hundred volumes for less than half their auction value.

With Jefferson's books as a nucleus, the library began to grow once more. By 1850 it contained some thirty-five thousand volumes. Then another setback occurred. On December 24, 1851, another disastrous fire consumed three-fifths of the stacks, including two-thirds of the now-precious Jefferson Collection. It was an unbelievable loss. But again, Congress passed an appropriation not only to replace them and house them in the West Wing of the Capitol but also to make the Library of Congress fireproof. By 1870, however, the library had grown in such enormous proportions that it had to have its own building. The library remained in the Capitol until the completion of the present Main Building in 1897. By 1930 even this proved inadequate to house its continued growth. In 1939 the first annex, the John Adams Building, was completed. The James Madison Memorial Building, a second major annex dedicated in 1980, is located on the south side of Independence Avenue.

The Library of Congress is now the world's largest library. According to its information office, the collections as of September 30, 1983, totaled a staggering 80 million items, filling more than 532 miles of shelves. In addition to over 20 million books and pamphlets, there are 50,000 bound newspaper volumes; nearly 40 million manuscripts; more than 3,800,000 maps and topographical views; 974,000 phonographic discs, tapes, and wires; 6 million pieces of music; 219,000 prints and drawings; 8,700,000 negatives, prints, and slides; 314,000 motion pictures; and 5,400,000 reels of microforms. Among its many treasures are a copy of the Gutenberg Bible, the Giant Bible of Mainz, drafts of Lincoln's Gettysburg Address, and Jefferson's draft of the Declaration of Independence.

The Thomas Jefferson Building is an outstanding example of Victorian architectural eclecticism. Countless motifs of literary, technological, and scientific achievement by over fifty painters, designers, and sculptors make it a museum of high Victorian art.

For those with less time, or who feel disinclined to suffer mental indigestion (we still have to take on the Capitol), I suggest that you stay with the highlights. We will therefore only visit the Great Hall and the Visitors' Gallery.

Enter the Library by the Main Entrance overlooking 1st Street and facing the Capitol *underneath* the entrance steps. You can either join the guided tour or enter the Great Hall or Main Entrance Hall.

The Great Hall is built of gleaming white Italian marble. In the center is a vast well enclosed in an arcade of two stories. On either side, north and south, is a massive staircase, richly ornamented with sculpture, the work of Phillip Martiny. The landing of each serves as a pedestal for figures of boys representing the four continents: America and Africa on the south side, and Europe and Asia facing the north. On the newel posts of each staircase are bronze female figures holding a cluster of electric lights. The balustrades at the top of the south staircase are ornamented with more figures of children representing comedy, poetry, and tragedy, with painting, architecture, and sculpture opposite.

In the ascending railing of the south staircase are more boys, representing occupations, habits, and pursuits. A mechanic, hunter, vintager, farmer, fisherman, soldier, chemist, and cook are seen here, while a gardener, entomologist, student, printer, musician, physician, electrician, and astronomer enliven the north balustrade.

And there's more to come. Each corner of the curved ceiling contains two female half-figures, also by Martiny, supporting a cartouche, showing a lamp and book, the symbols of learning. Higher up are flying geniuses, two in each corner, painted by Frederick C. Martin.

At the head of the staircase enter the Visitors' Gallery overlooking the great domed Main Reading Room or Rotunda, the very heart of the library. In this grandiose setting are 44,000 reference books for the use of readers and the huge card catalogue containing over 20 million cards indexing items in the library's collections in 468 languages. The dome, 100 feet in diameter, rises to 160 feet. In the collar and lantern of the dome are murals by Edwin Blashfield on the themes of the evolution of civilization and human understanding. Those in the collar consist of twelve seated figures, male and female, representing the twelve countries or epochs that have contributed most to the development of civilization—Egypt, *Written Records*; Judea, *Religion*; Greece, *Philosophy*; Rome, *Administration*; Islam, *Physics*; The Middle Ages, *Modern Languages*; Italy, *Fine Arts*; Germany, *Printing*; Spain, *Discovery*; England, *Literature*; France, *Emancipation*; and America, *Science*.

The ceiling of the lantern is depicted as sky and air, against which floats a female figure representing human understanding, attended by a pair of cherubic figures, or geniuses.

Atop each of the eight marble columns are sixteen portrait statues of men renowned in the field of knowledge. *Religion*, Moses and St. Paul (Charles H. Niehaus and John Donoghue); *Commerce*, Columbus and Robert Fulton (Paul W. Bartlett and Edward C. Potter); *History*, Herodotus and Gibbon (Daniel Chester French and Charles H. Niehaus); *Art*, Michelangelo and Beethoven (Paul W. Bartlett and Theodore Baur); *Philosophy*, Plato and Bacon (John J. Boyle); *Poetry*, Homer and Shakespeare (Louis St. Gaudens and Frederick McMonies); *Law,* Solon and Chancellor Kent (Wellington Rickstuhl and George Bissell); and *Science*, Newton and Joseph Henry (Cyrus E. Dallin and Herbert Adams).

The eight semicircular windows or lunettes above the reading room contain the seals of the forty-five states and three territories that made up the Union in 1897. The Great Seal of the United States is centered at the top of each stained-glass window.

As you exit the library by either of the side stairways, pause to look at the grottolike **Neptune Fountain*** (1897–1898, Rowland Hinton Perry), a flamboyant exercise in the manner of Bernini, a great Italian sculptor of the baroque period.

From here, turn right and continue north along 1st Street. Cross the street at the first stop light on the corner of East Capitol Street. Then continue west through the main entrance gate of the Capitol.

The Capitol

1st Street between Constitution Avenue and Independence Avenue, SE. Metro: Capitol South (1st and C and D). Open daily 9:00 A.M.–4:00 P.M. Closed Thanksgiving, Christmas, and New Year's. The Capitol Rotunda and Statuary Hall are open in the summer until 9:30 P.M. United States citizens may obtain Visitor Gallery passes from the offices of their Senator or Congressman. Foreign visitors may obtain passes to the Senate Gallery from the Senate sergeant-at-arms on the third floor; passports or other identification are required. For the House of Representatives, apply to the doorkeeper's office on the third floor. Free guided tours lasting 30 minutes leave every 3-4 minutes from the Rotunda, 9:00 A.M.–3:45 P.M. daily. Call

A short walk brings us to **The Capitol (3)**, one of the most imposing public buildings in the world, and also one of its most celebrated. Behind its massive Roman facades, House and Senate deliberate, debate, and decide policies that not only govern the United States of America, but concern the future of mankind everywhere.

Construction began in 1793 when Washington, escorted by his fellow Masons, laid the cornerstone. But it was not until 1803, when Jefferson appointed Latrobe surveyor of public buildings, that the many unresolved practical problems concerning its structure were resolved.

Thornton's original plan was impractical in almost every aspect. The Capitol should have been designed by L'Enfant, a trained architect and engineer. But after waiting for five months and *still* no designs from L'Enfant, Washington lost all patience and dismissed him. In a disappointing public competition of amateur and professional plans held in 1791, those of French architect Stephen Hallet were judged the best. But Dr. Thornton, a self-confessed amateur, submitted a more artistic design and Hallet was employed to make working drawings and supervise construction. Hallet, however, was accused of substituting his own plan for Thornton's and was dismissed in 1794. Hadfield succeeded him and met the same fate, as did James Hoban. The strong-minded Latrobe prevailed, however, and The Capitol was completed just before the War of 1812 broke out.

Under Latrobe's able direction the south wing was completed as an impressive legislative chamber resplendent with crimson draperies and exquisitely designed furniture. He also carried out a revision of Thornton's defective work in the north wing.

Tragically the war left most of this in ruins. In their article, "Latrobe's America" (*American Heritage*, August 1962), Norton and Halliday quote a story repeated by John Latrobe, the architect's son, about the British officer assigned to burn the House of Representatives who paused in the entrance in awe, to declare that it was "a pity to burn anything so beautiful." Mahogany chairs, desks, and tables were piled high and rockets fired. Similar measures were taken with the Senate wing and within minutes both wings were ablaze. Another young officer had rarely seen anything so grand and except for the burning of San Sebastian, could not recollect from any period of his life, a scene more striking or more sublime.

By July 1815, however, the indefatigable Latrobe was surveying the ruins and turning out plans for the reconstruction. It was at this time that he designed the famous tobacco capitals for the columns of the Senate rotunda, still a popular feature, as are the corncob capitals designed earlier for the Senate vestibule, outside the Old Supreme Court Chamber, which had miraculously survived the holocaust.

Somehow, in spite of the personal rivalries of its many architects, the burnings and reconstructions, and the endless modifications of Thornton's original design, The Capitol grew, undergoing further change, remodeling, and alteration through the nineteenth century to the present day. Charles Bulfinch (1763–1844) succeeded Latrobe and added a low dome and west front (1818–1829). Thomas U. Walter added new House and Senate wings and the present dome and supervised the placing of the huge bronze statue *Freedom* (1863, Thomas Crawford). Edward Clark contributed roof and skylight renovations, built terraces, and landscaped the grounds (1865–1902). David Lynn carried out the renovation of the House and Senate chambers, and George Stewart extended the east front and designed office buildings for the House and Senate (1954–1970).

The Capitol's grandeur owes a great deal to its distinctive features. The huge cupola is nearly the same size as that of St. Peter's in Rome. The main entrance to the interior is by lofty flights of steps. At the top of these, at either side, are two allegorical groups of sculpture representing *The Progress of Civilization* (1863, Thomas Crawford) on the Senate portico (east front). Notice also the Senate bronze doors (1868, Thomas Crawford) portraying scenes and events from George Washington's life and the struggle for independence.

The Capitol

Passing under the great colonnade, we enter the Rotunda, a vast circular hall enlivened by what Anthony Trollope thought "the worst pictures by which a nation ever sought to glorify its own deeds." The Capitol not only serves as the seat of Federal government but also as a museum filled

with works of art, some of considerable artistic merit and some definitely not. Besides paintings depicting great events of American history, it houses a collection of portraits and statues of Presidents, Vice-Presidents, Speakers, Senators, and others who have influenced the course of events. Statuary Hall, designed by Latrobe, located in what was the Old House of Representatives and one of the most elegant rooms of the original Capitol, contains statues of men selected by states as founding fathers or distinguished citizens.

Perhaps the most extraordinary works are the

battle scenes, allegorical figures, medallion portraits of national heroes, and major inventions created by Constantino Brumidi. Exiled from his native Rome, Brumidi, a professional muralist, came to Washington to become a U.S. citizen. Not only did he get his naturalization papers, but a commission to decorate the Agricultural Committee Room. The result, *Cincinnatus at the Plough*, was the first fresco ever painted in a public building on this side of the Atlantic. So pleased were all concerned that almost all the corridors and committee rooms were turned over to him. From 1855 to 1880, come what may, Civil War and the chaos of construction, the genial Brumidi at work became one of the sights of Washington. His masterwork, the *Apotheosis of Washington*, inside The Capitol dome itself, is a *tour de force* of Victorian art. Just as Michelangelo did in the Sistine Chapel, Brumidi lay on his back for eleven months. The work was completed in 1865. The original thirteen colonies surround Washington, who is flanked by representatives of liberty, victory, and fame. In the outer circle are the arts and sciences, marine, commerce, mechanics, agriculture, war, and freedom.

When he was over seventy, Brumidi undertook to decorate the frieze of the Rotunda. He had been working on it for three years and had got as far as Penn's Treaty with the Indians when he died as the result of a fall from the scaffolding. His assistant, Filippo Costaggini, worked from his sketches and continued the frieze illustration to the discovery of gold in California. About thirty feet of the frieze remained vacant until 1953 when Allyn Cox completed the last three scenes: the Civil War, the Spanish-American War, and the birth of aviation.

Retrace your steps to 1st Street. Turn left and walk a block to our next stop, the Supreme Court of the United States.

The Supreme Court

1st Street, NE. Metro: Capitol South (1st and C and D). Metrobus: take eastbound 30 from 10th Street and Pennsylvania Avenue to 1st and Independence Avenue, NE; or M6 from K Street to 1st Street and Constitution Avenue, NE. Open daily to the public Monday through Friday 9:00 A.M.–4:30 P.M. Closed Saturday, Sunday, and holidays. Free court room lectures every hour on the half-hour Monday through Friday 9:30 A.M.–3:30 P.M. when Court is not sitting (inquire from uniformed security police). Call (202)479-3499 to arrange group tours. The cafeteria on the ground floor is open to the public for breakfast and lunch.

On the west side of 1st Street, NE, opposite The Capitol, stands **The Supreme Court (4)**, with one of those heavy classical facades that Welsh poet Dylan Thomas, when visiting Washington for the first time in 1950, thought so incongruous in twentieth-century America.

Designed by Cass Gilbert, Jr. and John Rockart, the building is another exercise in which art and architecture combine to impress the viewer with the solemn, awesome power of government. Certainly they succeed. Low steps lead you up to a wide, oval plaza extending across the front of the building. On each side is an ornate flagpole with bronze and marble bases (1935, John Donnelly) with eagles atop, and a pair of marble candelabra with carved panels depicting *Justice* and the *Three Fates* (1935, John Donnelly). Then on each side of the precipitous main steps are huge marble seated figures (1935, James Earle Fraser). On the left is a brooding female figure representing *The Contemplation of Justice*. On the right is a male figure representing the *Authority of the Law*. Next are the sixteen huge Corinthian columns supporting an enormous portico. The sculptured pediment above illustrates the eloquent words below, "Equal Justice Under Law" (1935, Robert Aitkin), representing *Liberty Enthroned Guarded by Order and Authority*. In addition each side has a group of three figures depicting counsel and research.

The interior is no less grandiose. Gigantic bronze doors weighing thirteen tons slide into a wall recess when open. The low-relief panels (1935, John Donnelly) depict historic stages in the development of law. The main corridor, or Great Hall, is flanked by double rows of monolithic marble columns rising to a magnificently coffered ceiling. Busts of former chief justices are alternately set in niches and on

The Supreme Court

that sculpture played at a time when neoclassical and Beaux-Arts influences encouraged artists in the role of storyteller on a monumental scale.

Continue along 1st Street to Maryland Avenue, NE. Turn right and walk to the intersection of Maryland with Constitution Avenue. Just before the intersection is the **Mountjoy Bayly House (5)**, our next stop.

Mountjoy Bayly House

122 Maryland Avenue, NE. A National Historic Landmark. Private residence not open to the public.

We now enter a residential neighborhood of houses of different varieties and periods. Among them is the Mountjoy Bayly House, one of the earliest remaining dwellings in the Capitol Hill district. The handsome Federal house was built between 1817 and 1822 for Mountjoy Bayly, sergeant-at-arms and doorkeeper of the Senate. Unfortunately, Bayly bit off more than he could chew, as the saying goes. He never got full title due to his failure to pay off the mortgage for the land on which the house was built. The owner of the land was none other than Daniel Carroll of Duddington, the first of the Carrolls to own Capitol Hill, and one of the proprietors of land crucial for the construction of the Federal City. He foreclosed and sold the house to William J. McCormick, a lawyer.

The succession of owners that followed included a master butcher from the Old Center Market (which stood near the National Archives), a real estate agent, and another lawyer, before it became the home of Hiram Johnson, a controversial figure in his day. A staunch Republican Senator from California, Johnson commanded the forces of isolationism. He is perhaps best remembered as one of the "little group of willful men," as the disappointed Woodrow Wilson called him, who successfully killed American participation in the League of Nations, the short-lived precursor of the United Nations Organization.

When the house was remodeled in the Victorian style in the 1870s a mansard roof was added. When the Johnsons owned the house, between 1929 and 1945, it was restored to the elegance of the Federal era. Much of the interior colonial revival woodwork dates from this restoration. The double stairs with

bases along the side walls. The frieze is embellished with medallion profiles of illustrious lawgivers and heraldic devices.

From the Great Hall, we enter the Court Chamber, a large dignified room lined with marble Ionic columns and decorated with sculptured panels. These panels depict a medley of historic lawgivers and figures representing the rights of the people, wisdom, statecraft, fame, history, liberty, peace, and philosophy. The powers of good (security, harmony, peace, charity, and virtue) confront the powers of evil (corruption, slander, deceit, and despotic power).

Further features of the building include justices' chambers, conference rooms, and countless offices for the marshal of the court, law clerks, and secretaries, and four courtyards. Despite its ambience of pomp and circumstance, the Supreme Court Building expresses much of the essentially watchdog role of the Supreme Court—that of balancing society's need for order and the individual's right to freedom. It also reminds us of the immensely important part

Mountjoy Bayly House

cast-iron railings leading to the pedimented doorcase were also added by the Johnsons. After the death of her husband, Mrs. Johnson sold the house to the Federal Council of Churches of Christ in America. The house served as the headquarters for the General Commission on Chaplains and Armed Forces Personnel. The house has now been divided into apartments.

Continue down Maryland Avenue. Pause to view the historic Alva Belmont House, which stands opposite on the north side of the junction of Constitution and Maryland Avenues.

Alva Belmont House

144 Constitution Avenue and 2nd Street, NE. A National Historic Landmark owned by the National Women's Party. Telephone: (202)546-3989. Open Tuesday through Friday 10:00 A.M.–3:00 P.M. and Saturday, Sunday and holidays 12:00 NOON–4:00 P.M. Closed Thanksgiving, Christmas and New Year's.

The **Alva Belmont (6)**, or Sewall-Belmont House, is the headquarters of the National Women's Party,

Alva Belmont House

founded by suffragist Alice Paul, who wrote the Equal Rights Amendment in 1923. It is thought to be the oldest building on Capitol Hill and was declared a National Historic Landmark by an Act of Congress in 1974. Thousands of visitors to the nation's capital tour the House to view the memorabilia and antiques of suffrage and equal rights, as well as other historic memorabilia.

Certainly the Sewall-Belmont House is one of the city's most historic houses. The land was part of that granted to the second Lord Baltimore by King Charles in 1632. In 1799, Daniel Carroll sold it to Robert Sewall, who built a house on the property. The house was burned by the British on August 24–25, 1814, after a party of soldiers, sailors, and marines led by Cockburn and Major-General Robert Ross were suddenly fired on from the house. Four men were hit, one killed, and Ross had his horse shot dead from under him. "Splinters flew," writes Walter Lord in his *Dawn's Early Light* (1972), "as Lieutenant Scott led the party that broke through Sewall's front door. But it took several minutes, and by the time the men got in, the house was completely empty." Most accounts attribute the resistance to a group of diehard patriots led by a local barber named Dixon.

The house was rebuilt by Sewall and remained in the possession of his descendants for well over a century; one of these became the wife of John Strode Barbour, an influential Democratic Senator from Virginia. Then in 1922 the old house was bought by Porter H. Dale, Senator from Vermont, who restored both house and grounds to something like their former glory. The house now serves as headquarters for the National Women's Party, which named it the Alva Belmont House in honor of Mrs. Oliver H. P. Belmont, who helped them acquire the property.

Its most celebrated occupant was Gallatin, Secretary of the Treasury under Jefferson and Madison. Many of the discussions between Jefferson and his cabinet colleagues took place in the house. During his residence, 1801–1813, the canny Gallatin transacted the negotiations that led to the Louisiana Purchase, ending forever France's dream of controlling the Mississippi Valley, and beginning the expansion destined to carry the American flag to the Pacific. By means of a treaty and two conventions, the United States paid $11.25 million for a tract of 828,000 square miles lying between the Mississippi and the Rockies, setting aside an additional $3.75 million to settle the claims of its own citizens against France. Surely one of the biggest bargains in the history of real estate!

Proceed now to 2nd Street. Turn right and walk to A Street. Turn left on A and walk a block to the Museum of African Art, the **Home of Frederick Douglass (7).**

National Museum of African Art (and Home of Frederick Douglass)

318 A Street, NE. Telephone: (202)287-3490. Metro: Capitol South (1st and C and D, SE). Union Station (1st and Massachusetts, NE). Open Monday through Friday 10:00 A.M.– 5:00 P.M., Saturday and Sunday 12:00 NOON–5:00 P.M. Closed Christmas. Free. Gallery tours: Saturday and Sunday 12:30– 4:30 P.M.; special tours, call (202)287-3490, ext. 41 to request registration form. On weekends call (202) 357-2700. Time: 20 minutes.

The National Museum of African Art is the only museum in the United States devoted solely to the collection, study, and exhibition of African art. It is currently located in a series of townhouses on Capitol Hill, including the first Washington home of the noted nineteenth-century American abolitionist, Frederick Douglass.

In 1979 the museum merged with the Smithsonian Institution and in 1986 it is destined to take its place among the other Smithsonian museums on the Mall when the Center for African, Near Eastern, and Asian Cultures opens.

318 A Street is the first Washington home of Frederick Douglass (1817–1895). Runaway slave, abolitionist, editor, civil servant, and diplomat, Douglass was the outstanding Afro-American leader of the nineteenth century, the father of the civil rights movement.

Born Frederick Augustus Washington Bailey, a slave on Maryland's Eastern Shore, he learned to read and write at an early age. At twenty-one he ran away from his master in Baltimore and fled to the North, where he married and changed his name to Douglass. In 1845 he traveled to England where Quakers bought his freedom. Returning to the United States in 1847, he became a well-known lecturer, a leader of the Underground Railroad, and editor of *North Star*, an abolitionist newspaper. During the Civil War Douglass promoted the idea of black regiments, and two of his sons served in the Union Army.

In his later years Douglass, as one of the first blacks appointed to public office, served successfully as District of Columbia marshal, District of Columbia recorder, and U.S. minister to Haiti. He came to Washington as editor of the *New National Era* and bought the house on A Street in 1872. He lived here with his first wife, Anna Murray, until 1878, when he moved across the Anacostia River to Cedar Hill (1411 W Street, SE), now the Frederick Douglass Memorial Home, a museum run by the National Park Service.

The walk ends at the Museum of African Art. But for those who have the time and would like to see more of Capitol Hill, this optional side excursion to visit Eastern Market, Christ Church, and the Congressional Cemetery won't take more than two more hours. If you *don't* wish to take it, retrace your steps to Independence Avenue and take a westbound bus back to our starting point, the Bartholdi Fountain.

National Museum of African Art (Home of Frederick Douglass)

Eastern Market

7th Street and North Carolina Avenue, SE. Metro: Eastern Market (Pennsylvania and 7th). Open Tuesday through Thursday 7:00 A.M.–6:00 P.M., Friday and Saturday 6:00 A.M.–7:00 P.M., closed Sunday, Monday, and holidays.

As you leave the Museum of African Art, turn left down A Street, and walk south on 7th to the junction of Independence and North Carolina Avenues. On the far side of the intersection is **Eastern Market (8)**, one of the two remaining markets of Victorian Washington (it was established in 1802) and still thriving.

The present building, erected in 1873, was designed by Adolph Cluss (1825–1905), the architect of many of Washington's public buildings during the years of intensive construction 1862–1877.

Some of these have long since been demolished, for example Center Market, which stood on the site now occupied by the National Archives. But Masonic Hall, Catholic University, the Army Medical Museum, Calvary Baptist Church (see page 38), and The Smithsonian's Arts and Industries Building survive, as do Washington's Victorian public schools—Franklin, Jefferson, Curtis, Wallach, and Sumner.

Eastern Market itself is a barnlike structure with large bull's-eye windows alternating with arched windows and decorative brickwork. The market is at its liveliest on Saturday morning when truck farmers line the stalls outside to sell every variety of homegrown produce. Inside, old-fashioned propeller fans rotate over counters filled with fresh meat, fish, fruit, and vegetables.

Cluss was born in Würtemburg, Germany, where he began his studies. During the 1840s he trained

Eastern Market

in Brussels, where he met and became a friend of none other than Karl Marx. Between 1848 and 1850 he emigrated to the United States and worked briefly for the U.S. Coastal Survey before moving on to the office of the supervising architect of the Treasury and the Navy Yard, where he designed and built the furnaces that cast the navy's cannon.

Cluss lived a double life. In his student days he was a member of Marx's Communist Correspondent's Committee. In Washington he maintained his connection by translating Marx's articles to send to Marx's agent, for publication in the *New York Tribune,* for whom Marx wrote a weekly column.

By 1859, however, such anti-establishment activities had come to an end. Cluss was now happily

married to a nice German girl from Baltimore who appears to have firmly discouraged such activities. He collaborated with Von Kammerhueber to design the Masonic Hall (see page 35) and went on to pioneer a series of still-standing public schools, each incorporating ornate multicolored brickwork and elaborate cast-iron columns that occasionally doubled as heat pipes.

Cluss caught the friendly eye of Boss Shepherd and was his architect for a real estate development, an elegant row of mansions that stood at Connecticut Avenue and K Street on the north side of the newly landscaped Farragut Square. Shepherd was both praised and damned for the improvements he made. But the city was made almost bankrupt in

the process. Ironically, during the congressional investigations into Shepherd's mishandling of Federal funds, Cluss testified against him. Cluss said he had been ordered to authorize false quantity measurements and compared Shepherd to New York's Boss Tweed. Cluss hadn't lost all his youthful idealism. After this he went from strength to strength. He designed Catholic University, rebuilt the inside of the burnt-out Patent Office (see page 36), and created his masterpiece, the Smithsonian's Arts and Industries Building.

Continue on 7th Street across Pennsylvania Avenue to G Street. Turn right on G and walk a block to **Christ Church***, G Street, SE. Services: Sundays 8:30 A.M. and 11:00 A.M. Visitors welcome. For

visits during the week, inquire at the office, next door to the church.

Founded in 1794, Christ Church was first housed in Daniel Carroll's tobacco barn, then on Capitol Hill at New Jersey Avenue. The present building, designed by Latrobe, but much altered, was completed in 1807. His daughter, Lydia, who shocked her parents by falling in love at thirteen with Nicholas Roosevelt (a greatuncle of Teddy Roosevelt) was married to Roosevelt here in 1808.

John Philip Sousa, the celebrated bandmaster and composer, was born on the same block as Christ Church and was also married here; he is buried in its graveyard, **Congressional Cemetery***, 18th and E Streets, SE. A National Historic Landmark. Metro: Stadium or Army, (19th and C) or Potomac Avenue (14th and G). Open daily 9:00 A.M.–4:30 P.M. Free. Visitors should inquire at the gatekeeper's house for information and maps to locate grave sites.

Congressional Cemetery is not, and never was, officially *the* congressional cemetery. It was established in 1807 by a group of Capitol Hill residents who in 1812 turned it over to Christ Church, which still owns it. By 1816, however, so many Senators, Congressmen, officials, and prominent citizens were buried here that Congress was compelled to give Christ Church occasional grants of financial aid to reserve a section of the 30-acre burial ground for the interment of VIPs. Among the famous resting here are: Tobias Lear, beloved friend and private secretary of Washington; the architects Thornton, Mills, Hadfield, and Latrobe; Mathew Brady; Pushmataha, the Choctaw chief who fought under Jackson against the British in the Pensacola campaign; and J. Edgar Hoover, once all-powerful chief of the Federal Bureau of Investigation. Some seventy-five Congressmen, and fifty-five Senators are buried here, most under cenotaphs designed by Latrobe. The use of these distinctive monuments ceased in 1877 after a caustic philistine speech by Senator Hoar of sachusetts. "Being interred beneath them," he quipped, "added a new terror to death."

Congressional Cemetery is noted for its sculptured tombs. It was to have been America's Westminster Abbey, but railroads made it possible to bury VIPs in their local cemeteries. Today, the cemetery seems all but forgotten and most of its eighty thousand graves are neglected, although restoration is planned.

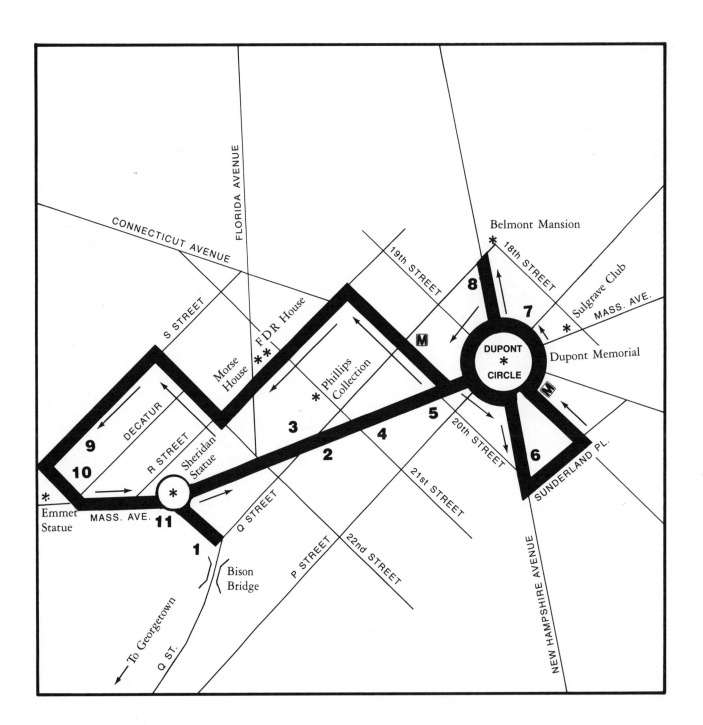

The Mansions of Massachusetts Avenue

Distance: 2–3 miles. Time: 2–3 hours, depending on how many houses visited. Metro: Dupont Circle (Dupont Circle and 19th). Metrobus: westbound D2, D4 (22nd and P Streets, NW), N2 or N4 (Sheridan Circle). Parking: commercial lots on P Street and Connecticut Avenue. Restaurants: along Connecticut Avenue to the north of Dupont Circle there are many inexpensive light-food establishments, including the excellent Kramer Bookshop cafés at 1347 and 1117 Connecticut Avenue, NW.

The mansions of Massachusetts Avenue and the streets adjacent to it take us back to Washington's *belle époque*, an ostentatious era of high living that followed the Spanish-American War of 1898 and ended with the Great Depression.

Laid out gradually from 1890, from Scott Circle westward to Dupont Circle and on to Sheridan Circle, Massachusetts Avenue became the longest and grandest of the capital's boulevards; some three hundred ornate mansions had been built along its corridor by the time the United States entered World War I in 1917. Taxes were low and assessments moderate. To the city came merchant princes from New York and New England, industrialists and railroad tycoons from Pennsylvania and Ohio, lumber barons and mineowners from the Far West, meatpackers and newspaper magnates from the Midwest. All vied with one another to build palaces, villas, and mansions, occupied in some instances, only during the Washington winter season. These newly rich Americans and their descendants flourished in their private *palazzi* until the prolonged effect of the 1929 crash finally forced many of them to sell to buyers for use as embassies, offices, or clubs.

The four mansions open to the public will enable you to savor this bygone lifestyle. The magnificent Anderson House is headquarters of *The Society of the Cincinnati* and a national museum of memorabilia and relics relating to the Revolution. The brownstone Phillips Mansion, originally the family residence of Cleveland industrialist James Laughlin Phillips, now houses the famous Phillips Collection. The Christian Heurich Memorial Mansion, a striking example of the high Victorian style, its shadowy rooms intact, is now the home of the Columbia Historical Society.

The extension of Massachusetts Avenue beyond Florida Avenue in the first decade of the twentieth century led to a second concentration of mansions, this one around and beyond Sheridan Circle. Taft, Harding, Wilson, Hoover, and Franklin D. Roosevelt, all past or future Presidents at the time, had bought houses in the Kalorama district bordering Massachusetts Avenue on the north. Here is located the fourth mansion open to the public, the Woodrow Wilson House, home of President and Mrs. Wilson from the end of his last term in 1921 until his death in 1924, and now a house museum administered by the National Trust for Historic Preservation.

Although the majority of the great mansions on Massachusetts Avenue are not open to the general public, special one-day tours are occasionally sponsored by the Davis Memorial Goodwill Industries (annually in May), the National Trust, Smithsonian Associates, and the Dupont Circle Citizens' Association. Between such occasions you can only gaze at the grand facades or peek through ground-floor windows and front doors and feel thankful that they have at least been given a new lease on life.

Everett House

1606 23rd Street, NW. A National Historic Landmark owned by the Republic of Turkey. Not open to the public.

The sculptured Bison Bridge buffaloes and Indian heads (1914, Alexander Phimester) at 23rd and Q Streets, NW, mark the starting point of our tour. Turn north on 23rd and walk toward the equestrian statue of Civil War hero General Philip Sheridan,

Everett House (Turkish Embassy)

standing, to quote Hugh Jacobsen, like a mounted policeman directing traffic. Immediately on the left, rising in the air like the Ark, is the palatial **Everett House** (1), now the Turkish Embassy.

The architect of this impressive structure was George Oakley Totten, Jr. (1886–1939), who in the early decades of the century designed a baker's dozen of such mansions in Washington. Totten designed the house (completed 1914) for Edward H. Everett, a Cleveland multimillionaire industrialist and inventor of the crimped Coca-Cola bottle cap. Combining various elements of the Renaissance style, he lavished the facade with every feature of a European palace. Behind the huge entrance hall of black-and-white marble, one finds gold-plated door knobs, elaborately carved beams, brocaded walls, a musicians' gallery, a paneled ballroom complete with stage and fluted columns, a conservatory and loggia, a pillared drawing room, a rococo Otis elevator, twelve or so bedrooms, and even a swimming pool in the basement, not to mention the patent Webster air washer and humidifier.

Until Everett's death in 1929, the great mansion was the scene of numerous social events. Seated on gold-painted art nouveau bentwood chairs, more than one hundred guests frequently listened to celebrated prima donnas fresh from triumphs at the Metropolitan Opera. Everett was survived by his second wife, Grace, who occupied the house until the fall of 1932 when the chairs mysteriously vanished. The house was rented to the Turkish embassy in 1932 and bought by the Turkish government in 1936. For some years afterward, the chairless embassy rented chairs at $2.50 each for its musical *soirées*. That is, until the wife of the present Turkish ambassador decided to take matters into her own hands. She searched the attics, where she discovered a great canvas-covered heap. Underneath the covering were the missing ballroom chairs, which ever since have performed their original function.

The Society of the Cincinnati (Anderson House)

2118 Massachusetts Avenue, NW. A National Historic Landmark owned by The Society of the Cincinnati. Telephone: (202)785-0540. Open Tuesday through Saturday 1:00–4:00 P.M. Closed on Federal holidays and Saturdays July through August. Self-guided tour. Time: 1 hour.

Continue east from Sheridan Circle, down Massachusetts Avenue to 22nd Street. Directly on the right, between 22nd and 21st Streets you will see the twin arches and carriage court of **Anderson House (2)**, international headquarters and museum of The Society of the Cincinnati.

Anderson House was the Washington residence of Larz Anderson and his heiress wife, Isabel. It was built between 1902 and 1906 at an estimated cost of $800,000. The architects were Arthur Little (1852–1925) and Herbert W. C. Browne (1860–1946) of Boston.

Larz Anderson (1866–1937) was a prominent diplomat and held as his most important posts the positions of envoy extraordinary and plenipotentiary to Belgium, and ambassador to Japan. After his death Mrs. Anderson gave the house to The Society of the Cincinnati, a patriotic organization in which both were actively involved.

At this point, you may ask, *what* is The Society of the Cincinnati? Founded in 1783 by a group of officers of the Continental Army before their demobilization after the Revolutionary War, the society was fraternal and nonpolitical, taking its name from

Cincinnatus, a Roman patriot who, according to tradition, was called in 458 B.C. from farm and family to save the Roman republic but returned to his farm afterward. Membership was limited to officers and their eldest male descendants. Glance up at the pediment over the portico of the main entrance. Emblazoned there are the arms of the Cincinnati, the insignia designed by L'Enfant and allowed to be worn by its members.

Inside, the old mansion looks somewhat like the set of a Vincent Price melodrama. The more interesting of the society's collections are devoted to the Revolutionary period. The musty rooms, crammed with treasures of bronze and brass, marble and stone, as well as gold and silver, tend to be travelers' pieces on the whole, fascinating as some items so undoubtedly are.

If you want to learn more about the society and its collections, read James Orr Denby's *The Society of the Cincinnati and Its Museum* (Society of the Cincinnati, 1967). But until you do, I hope the following outline will serve as an appetizer.

A marble bust of Washington greets us on entry. He was the first president-general of the society. Around the entrance hall are the flags of the original thirteen states, France, and the society, the last distinguished by the horizontal blue and white stripes.

Turn right and walk through the archway to the Choirstall Room, so called because of the choirstall paneling from an unknown Italian Renaissance church. The flags here are copies of the colors carried by the French regiments who helped American troops fight the British during the final phase of the Revolution.

Walk now through the doorway at the west end of the Great Stairhall, which is used primarily for changing exhibits. The hall also contains portraits of French military and naval leaders, including Admiral de Grasse, and Counts Rochambeau and d'Aboville. Note the walls, which are decorated in the remarkable technique of *trompe l'oeil* ("fool-the-eye"), to give the impression of a sculptured effect.

Through the door to the left of the fireplace we pass decorated alcoves containing busts of Washington and Nicholas Longworth, the maternal great-grandfather of Larz Anderson. The sculptor of Washington's bust is unknown. The second, of horticulturist Nicholas Longworth (1782–1863) of Cincinnati, Ohio, is an early work by Hiram Powers (1805–1873). Longworth, the first millionaire of

The Society of the Cincinnati (Anderson House)

what was then the West, established the vineyards of the Ohio Valley before California ever thought of raising the grape.

Now enter the former Billiard Room. The paintings hung here, portraits by American artists, represent members of the society, including an interesting portrait of Colonel Richard Clough Wheeler. The Colonel was the great-grandfather of Larz and served as aide-de-camp to Lafayette. The glass cases contain a changing collection of Revolutionary War Medals, watches, and swords once worn by celebrated commanders.

Retrace your steps to the stairhall and proceed up the stone staircase. On the first landing, we pass a very large and impressive painting, entitled *The Triumph of the Dogaressa Anna Marie Foscari in the Year 1424*. Painted by the Spanish artist José Villegas, the subject represents an incident from the proces-

Society of the Cincinnati (Larz Anderson House)

Generals Greene and Wayne, Major General von Steuben, and Colonel Anderson. Dove in hand, the goddess of peace (the model was the radiant Mrs. Anderson) sheathes the sword of the goddess of war. On the opposite side of the room another design concerns the Civil War. In the distance lie Charleston Harbor and Fort Sumter. At the outbreak of the war, the fort was commanded by a great-uncle of Larz, Major Robert Anderson, United States Army, who spiked the guns of Fort Moultrie, moved his small garrison to the more defensible Fort Sumter, and found himself catapulted to fame as the hero of the hour.

Exit through the door on the right, by the window, to the French Parlor. Elaborately decorated in Louis XV style, it bears paneling and plaster decorations made after the ambassador's own designs. In the glass case are examples of Ming jade trees of the late nineteenth century.

Continue to the English Parlor, so called because of the many pictures painted by English artists. Notice the fine portrait of the Countess Dundonald by Sir Henry Raeburn. The handsome Chippendale-style furniture is American, and there is a set of small French chairs, each upholstered with a scene representing a fable from Aesop.

Return now to the French Parlor through the door on the right. Turn right into the Long Gallery hung with three huge sixteenth-century Brussels Diana tapestries (there are more in the Dining Room ahead). These were once owned by Cardinal Francesco Barberini (1597–1679), who received them from Louis XIII of France. On various chests and tables and in cabinets are more trophies and objects collected by the Andersons on their global travels between 1914 and 1934.

Walk through the doorway at the end of the gallery and turn right into the Dining Room. Paneled in the seventeenth-century style of Grinling Gibbons, this contains more objects and more memorabilia, notably portraits of the tall, distinguished Larz as ambassador and the beautiful Mrs. Anderson. The latter, by Cecilia Beaux (1855–1942), is an especially fine example of this now largely forgotten painter and her vital yet restrained style. The remaining tapestries are to be seen here, as well as a remarkable eight-fold Chinese screen with porcelain plaques representing various historical episodes.

Pass through either of the doors on the west side and enter the great Ballroom through the Musicians' Gallery. Above the gallery is a fine double portrait of

sion of a newly elected doge of Venice on the day of inauguration.

Through the right-hand doorway at the top of the stairs we now enter the Key Room, distinguished by allegorical murals by H. Siddons Mowbray (1858–1928), representing various events in the history of the United States and the Anderson family. One of these depicts Washington presenting a diploma of the society to Lafayette in the presence of the Andersons by one of the most fashionable portraitists of the 1920s and '30s, the Hungarian Phillip de Lazlo.

Return now to the Long Gallery, turn right, and descend the stairs to the ground floor. Lining the staircase to the entrance hall and around the walls of the hall itself are portraits (good, bad, and indifferent, representing a wide range of professional portrait styles) of former president-generals of the society. Continue through the door to the left at the foot of the stairs and enter the Ballroom proper. Used for a variety of prestigious social functions, this huge room can be fully appreciated only on those splendid occasions when the society holds white-tie soirées. Over the ornate fireplace is a portrait of Henry Knox, founder of the society, flanked by a pair of Japanese Imari jars. Chinese Buddhist statues look down from niches around the walls, and at the west end of the handsome room is a six-fold painted leather Coromandel screen.

You have yet to see the Solarium, entered on the south side of the ballroom. Here, more murals depict the favorite automobile routes of the Andersons. The room at the east end was the breakfast room; its walls are decorated with paintings of the gardens of the Andersons' summer residence, "Weld," in Brookline, Massachusetts, named for Isabel's illustrious maternal Boston ancestors.

Continue to the Library, our last stop. Gilbert Stuart's fine portrait of General Horatio Gates immediately attracts the eye. Opposite, to the left of the fireplace, is an endearing portrait of Larz Anderson's father, Nicholas Longworth Anderson, one of the younger Union generals of the Civil War, and above the fireplace is Larz Anderson in diplomatic uniform by DeWitt Lockman.

Cosmos Club (Townsend Mansion)

2121 Massachusetts Avenue, NW. A National Historic Landmark owned by the Cosmos Club. Not open to the public.

As you walk out of Anderson House, look across Massachusetts Avenue at the ornate Louis XVI-style facade opposite. This is the **Cosmos Club (3)**, one of the world's most famous clubs, a meeting place of distinguished men (and, occasionally, women) in science, literature, and the fine arts. Founded in 1878 by John Wesley Powell (1834–1902), the celebrated geologist and explorer, the club moved here in 1952 from the Cutts-Madison House (see page 24).

Formerly the Townsend residence, the mansion is intimately associated with Franklin D. Roosevelt and his circle before he entered the White House as President in 1933. From 1925 it was the home of Sumner Welles (1892–1961), diplomat and architect of the Roosevelt administration's Good Neighbor Policy with Latin America. Welles had inherited the house from a former wife, Mathilde Scott Townsend, daughter of Richard and Mary Townsend, the original builders and first occupants. The immensely wealthy Richard H. Townsend (1850–1902) was president of the Erie and Pittsburgh Railroad before retiring and moving to Washington. His wife, Mary, every bit as rich, was the daughter of Tom Scott of the Pennsylvania Railroad.

Mary, who died in 1931, was an heiress of great beauty and lived "a life strewn with roses," to quote one interviewer of the Thirties. While still a young girl, she was told by a gypsy fortuneteller that if she ever ventured to live "under a new roof" she would die within six months. Accordingly, when the Townsends built the house, between 1899 and 1901, they commissioned architect John Merven Carrère (1858–1911) to design an elaborate mansion *around* the shell of the older Hillyer house. Mary thus escaped the dreaded prediction. Nonetheless, the prophecy did come true, but for her husband. Shortly after the house was completed, Richard fell from his horse, fatally fracturing his skull.

Although a certain amount of the original interior has disappeared as the result of remodeling to adapt the building for the various functions of a prestigious private club, it remains essentially as it was during the occupancy of the Townsends and the Welleses. Notably the same are the impressive entrance hall embellished with a gray-veined white-marble floor and the library with its enormous fireplace mantel, a plaster copy of the original at the Château of Blois, France. Much of Olmstead's original landscaping disappeared in 1952 to make way for additions and the inevitable parking lot, but the incredible wealth of decorative features—friezes,

Cosmos Club (Townsend Mansion)

brass hardware, lunettes, and doorways—make the former Townsend mansion a museum of the decorative arts of the Edwardian era.

Continue down Massachusetts Avenue to 21st Street. Facing us on the southeast corner of Massachusetts and 21st are the porte-cochere and the undulating walls of another palatial mansion, the former **Walsh-McLean House (4)**, now the Indonesian Embassy, our next stop.

Walsh-McLean House

2020 Massachusetts Avenue, NW. A National Historic Landmark owned by the Republic of Indonesia. Generally not open to the public, but can occasionally be visited on embassy tours.

Irishman Thomas Francis Walsh, a farmer's boy from Clonmel, County Tipperary, had risen rapidly in the world when he built this fabulous sixty-room man-

Walsh-McLean House (Indonesian Embassy)

sion. His was the classic story of local boy making good, or, easy come, easy go. In 1869, at the age of nineteen, he had emigrated to the United States. Two years later he moved from Worcester, Massachusetts, to Golden, Colorado, where he built bridges for the Colorado Central Railroad, studying geology in his spare time. He made a fortune in the Black Hills Gold Rush (1876) and the Leadville Gold Rush some years later, only to lose it all in the recession of 1893. But the discovery of the Camp Bird Mine at Quray, Colorado, made him the sole owner of one of the world's richest gold mines. His

daughter, Evalyn, never forgot that day. Father called her into his bedroom and whispered in her ear, "I've struck it rich!" Camp Bird Mine produced $5,000 a day. Walsh sold the mine in 1902 for $43 million plus twenty-five percent of the profits from the ore for $2 million more, as well as $100,000 in stock.

By this time, Tom and his growing family had shaken the dust and mud of the mining camps off their feet and moved on to Washington. After buying publisher Conrad Miller's house at 1825 Phelps Place, NW (now the office of the Soviet Embassy's agricultural counsellor), Tom decided the time was ripe to impress the world with his wealth. He bought land on Massachusetts Avenue and in 1901 hired New York architect Henry Anderson to design not only the biggest but the very finest mansion on the avenue. Anderson certainly responded to the challenge by combining Renaissance, baroque, *and* rococo within an art nouveau framework.

Tom Walsh's dream house is every bit as big and impressive as he hoped it would be. It contains more than fifty rooms, including an incredible three-story galleried stairhall roofed over with stained glass and embellished with a sinuously curved art nouveau mahogany balustrade. The balustrade was a feature Walsh had copied from the grand stairway on the White Star liner that had taken the family to Europe in 1897 after McKinley appointed Tom a commissioner to the Paris Exposition.

The wealth and the power that went with his money naturally became a Washington legend. One cab driver, guiding tourists along Massachusetts Avenue, stopped outside to inform everyone that the house was the "five million dollar home of the Colorado Monte Cristo." Daughter Evalyn, however, thought this an exaggeration. In her book *Father Struck It Rich* (1936), she wrote that the house cost $835,000. But this was exclusive of contents: costly rugs from Bokhara and Smyrna; paintings, sculpture, and objets d'art from Paris, London, and Brussels; plus shiploads of fine furniture from the palaces and workshops of Europe; not to mention the gold dinner service made from nuggets taken from Camp Bird Mine, made the cab driver's guess a very conservative one.

During the Theodore Roosevelt administration (1901–1909), the Walsh mansion was the scene of the most lavish entertainment in Washington. At one New Year's Eve party, according to *The New York Times*, 325 guests consumed 480 quarts of champagne, 288 fifths of Scotch, 48 quarts of cocktails, 40 gallons of beer, and 35 bottles of liqueurs. A dinner party of less than fifty guests was considered an intimate affair. Guests at various balls and banquets included Presidents Theodore Roosevelt, Taft, Wilson, and Harding; Admiral Dewey; King Albert and Queen Elizabeth of the Belgians; and the Duke of Brabant, later King Leopold III of the Belgians, who invested in Walsh's mine.

Tom and Carrie Walsh enjoyed only a few happy years in the huge mansion. Their troubles began in 1905 when daughter Evalyn was badly injured and son Vinson killed in an automobile accident. Tom, once a gregarious crony of powerful politicans, became increasingly withdrawn. When he died in 1910, his skin and the whites of his eyes had yellowed like the gold that had made him so rich. Evalyn herself had more than her share of misfortune. Two years before, in 1908, she had eloped with Edward Beale ("Ned") McLean, whose family owned *The Cincinnati Enquirer* and *The Washington Post*.

Young McLean was even more of a big spender than Evalyn. As soon as they were married, the McLeans took off on a worldwide honeymoon-*cum*-buying extravaganza. The two fathers put up $100,000 each for the "young couple to enjoy themselves." In those days, Cleveland Amory reminds us, such a sum was almost unspendable. But spend it they did, and they even had to cable for more to cover their last hotel bill in Paris!

Although Evalyn's bad luck began before she acquired the supposedly unlucky Hope Diamond (to be seen in the Hall of Gems, Museum of Natural History, Washington, D.C.), superstitious friends blamed Evalyn's lifelong misfortunes on the legend of bad luck associated with the celebrated stone. Former proud possessors included Louis XVI and Marie Antoinette, and a long list of subsequent owners were either shot, driven to suicide or bankruptcy, or lost their reason. The McLean's first child, Vinson, known as the "one hundred million dollar baby," was killed by a passing car in 1919. Evalyn's beautiful daughter, Evalyn, at twenty became the fifth wife of the rakish fifty-seven-year-old Senator Roland Rice Reynolds of North Carolina and died of an alleged overdose of sleeping pills. Evalyn's own marriage disintegrated when Ned's drinking finally ended in insanity; hospitalized for eight years, he died of a heart attack in 1941. Evalyn herself also died in tragic circumstances.

Mrs. Tom Walsh had lived on in the great house until her death in 1932, and although Evalyn inherited the property, she couldn't bear to live there any longer. "It was cold," she wrote after a chance visit in 1937, "but its deepest chill lodged in my heart." In 1935 the house was rented to the Resettlement Administration, a New Deal agency. When the government moved out in 1937, the house remained empty until America entered World War II. Evalyn gave it rent free to the Red Cross for the duration. The Indonesian government purchased the house in 1951.

The great mansion no longer stands in all its former glory. The vast and ornate Louis XVI ballroom on the fourth floor, once resplendent with tapestries and gold brocade, is now partitioned into office space. Yet many of its rich trappings remain, if only partially obscured by the ambience of departed grandeur. And, according to Washington's ghost authority, Evalyn herself has returned at least in spirit. In his book, *Washington's Most Famous Ghost Stories* (1975), John Alexander wrote that a beautiful nude Evalyn has been seen sliding down the stairway hall just as she did as a girl!

Before continuing east down Massachusetts Avenue to our next stop, the Blaine Mansion, cross the avenue and walk a few steps up 21st Street. On your immediate left is the brownstone **Phillips Collection***, 1600–1612 21st Street, NW. Telephone: (202)387-0961. Open Tuesday through Saturday 10:00 A.M.–5:00 P.M., Sundays 2:00–7:00 P.M. Closed Mondays, New Year's Day, the Fourth of July, Thanksgiving, and Christmas. Free.

Rest your feet here. You can then decide whether or not to return and devote a morning or an afternoon to viewing the famous Phillips Collection acquired by Duncan Phillips and established in the house as a memorial to his brother and his father, Major Clinch Phillips, a Civil War veteran turned glass manufacturer. The mansion was opened to the public in 1921 by Duncan and his artist wife, the former Marjorie Acker, as the first museum of modern art in the United States. By 1930, because of the growth of the collection, the Phillipses moved to another house, and turned the 1897 brownstone over for museum use. The new gallery wing was added in 1960.

This highly personal but nonetheless superb collection is mainly French and American art of the nineteenth and twentieth centuries; some rooms are devoted entirely to such artists as Klee, Braque, Bonnard, and Rothko. There are important examples of the work of Degas, Gauguin, Matisse, Vuillard, Renoir, Van Gogh, Courbet, Chardin, Cézanne, Daumier, Eakins, Goya, Homer, Kokoschka, Modigliani, Picasso, Louis, and O'Keefe.

Blaine Mansion

2000 Massachusetts Avenue, NW. A National Historic Landmark owned by Samuel Spencer, Violet Spencer, and Roger Cortesi and adapted for professional office use. Not open to the public.

This brooding Victorian pile is the **Blaine Mansion (5)**. Standing on the south side of Massachusetts Avenue where the avenue and P Street converge at 20th, its vast red-brick bulk dominates the northwest approach. It was built in 1882 for James Gillespie Blaine (1830–1893), a prominent Republican who served variously as Speaker of the House, Senator from Maine, Secretary of State, and unsuccessful candidate for President. "Slippery Jim," as he was called, is perhaps best remembered as the unfortunate target of a celebrated *Puck* cartoon by Bernhard Gillam depicting his body tattooed with all the deals with which he was supposed to have been associated. His reputation as a wheeler-dealer, combined with failure to repudiate an anti-Catholic speech by a supporter, cost him the Presidency.

The huge mansion proved to be too costly to maintain. While Secretary of State, Blaine hired Philadelphia architect John Fraser (c. 1825–1903) to design the house. But Garfield's assassination on July 2, 1881, after only four months in the White House, brought Blaine's resignation. His wife, Harriet, deplored the mansion's enormous size even before its completion, complaining of its demands on her energies as well as the family budget. Blaine himself liked living here as it was close to the then wooded hills of Kalorama, and wrote his memoirs in its spacious library through the winter of 1882–1883.

Fraser, who designed the equally brooding Union League Club on Broad Street, Philadelphia, was typically high Victorian in that he blended a lively mix of Romanesque, Gothic, and Renaissance elements. Hipped towers dominate a cluster of chimneys and skylights topped with ornamental ironwork, weathervane, and lightning rods, finials, and spikes. Notice the Eastlake-style woodwork, especially the carriage porch with its turned clustered columns ornamented with intricate jigsaw panels—typical features of the style.

In 1883 the Blaines leased the house to the Chicago millionaire Levi Leiter, who lived here until his own palatial residence on Dupont Circle was com-

Blaine Mansion

pleted in 1894 (demolished in 1947 to build the Hotel Dupont Plaza). In 1898 the Blaine House was leased to George Westinghouse, celebrated inventor of the air brake who subsequently bought it and lived in it until his death in 1914. After many more changes of ownership, the mansion ceased to be a private residence and was converted for office use in 1948.

Leave Massachusetts Avenue via Dupont Circle and walk to P Street (in the direction of People's Drug). Cross P and turn right on New Hampshire Avenue. One block ahead, at the corner of New Hampshire and Sunderland Place, is the Heurich Mansion.

Christian Heurich Memorial Mansion

1307 New Hampshire Avenue, NW. A National Historic Landmark owned by the Columbia Historical Society. Telephone: (202)785-2068. Metro: Dupont Circle (Connecticut and Q). Open Friday and Saturday 12:00 NOON–4:00 P.M.; library open Wednesday, Friday, and Saturday 10:00 A.M.–4:00 P.M. Closed Federal holidays. Tours every thirty minutes (last tour 3:30 P.M.), $1.00. Time: 25 minutes.

The **Christian Heurich Memorial Mansion (6)**, a massive brownstone structure, whose style has been defined by architectural historian Richard Howland

Christian Heurich Memorial Mansion (Columbia Historical Society)

as "beer-barrel baronial," is the winter palace the Munsters might have been expected to rent for the Washington debut of *their* daughter. But it was home for many years for Christian Heurich, a German immigrant who made a fortune from a famous local lager beer brewed in an equally imposing establishment (demolished in 1962) in the Foggy Bottom district.

Heurich was a Washington legend and so was his mansion, a monument to his success and the good American life. Born in Haina-bei-Roemhild, Saxe-Meiningen, Germany, in 1842, he lived to the ripe old age of 102, drinking his lager beer to the end ("Recommended for Family Use by Physicians in General"). He seems to have been equally successful in his domestic life. "I was six times engaged," he wrote, "three times married, and each time happily."

After his death in 1945, Amelia, his third wife, presented the mansion to the Columbia Historical Society, which since 1956 has maintained it as its headquarters. The society, a nonprofit institution founded in 1894, is dedicated to the preservation and dissemination of information about the District of Columbia.

The Heurich Mansion, designed by John Grandville Meyers in Norman revival style, was completed in 1892. The first fireproof private residence in the city, it was designed with all the embellishments of Victorian architecture as decreed by John Ruskin. Gargoyles, turrets, frescoes, and lavish paneling abound. The interior is gloomily grand, with a series of ornately furnished rooms that include a music room overhung with a mezzanine gallery. A gigantic gas lamp stands at the foot of an opulent staircase of brass, marble, and onyx. And don't be startled by the suit of armor guarding the hall as you enter. In the conservatory, a fountain, a memorial to a daughter who died in childhood, lends an air of melancholy enchantment to the already oppressive ambience.

In contrast, you may find the most interesting room to be the basement German breakfast room, decorated with mural paintings of beer steins and happy inbibers. Above the fireplace on the ceiling is the Latin motto, *Gaudeamus igitur* ("Therefore let us rejoice") backed up by folksy German sayings on the walls, extolling the sustaining qualities of good beer. On the left-hand side of the fireplace is *Raum ist in der kleinsten Kammer für den grossten Katzenjammer* ("There is room in the smallest chamber for the biggest hangover"). Others include, *Schopf aus ein Pokale neue Ideale* ("Draw new ideals from your drinking cup"); *Eine guter Trunk macht alt Leute jung* ("A good drink makes old people young"); and *Eine froher Gast ist niemand's Last* ("A happy guest is nobody's burden").

If one can believe that the inside of any house does acquire a sense of intimacy and secrecy, real or imagined, because of what seems to have happened in it, then certainly the Heurich Mansion is haunted. Perhaps it is from the unique personality of Heurich himself that his mansion acquired its strange mix of Gothic *gemütlichkeit*, reflecting his ideas, emotions, and wanderlust, tempered with a dauntless *bonhomie*.

Patterson House

15 Dupont Circle, NW. A National Historic Landmark owned by the Washington Club. Not open to the public.

As you stagger out from under the porte cochere of the Heurich Mansion, turn left and walk up New Hampshire Avenue to Dupont Circle. Cross over to the park itself to view the Patterson House, an imposing white marble Renaissance palace on the northeast corner of Dupont Circle and P Street. The Washington Club, a prominent women's organization, occupies this former home of Eleanor ("Cissy") Patterson, one time owner of the daily Washington *Times-Herald* and daughter of Robert Wilson Patterson and heiress Elinor Medill Patterson.

Before you approach the house, however, look at the elegant **Samuel F. Dupont Memorial Fountain***. Congress honored Admiral Samuel Francis Dupont (1803–1865) for his services in the Civil War by naming the intersection of Massachusetts and Connecticut Avenues Dupont Circle and placed a small standing figure of the naval warrior in the middle. But the Dupont family wanted something grander and pressured Congress to allow a more artistic memorial to be built at family expense. Sculptor Daniel Chester French (1850–1931) was commissioned in 1917 to execute the figures representing sky, wind, and sea in a suitable setting designed by architect Henry Bacon.

Over the years, the neighborhood has changed a great deal. When the monument was completed in 1921, the Dupont Circle area was residential, and

Patterson House (Washington Club)

adjacent buildings were Renaissance, Second Empire, or Beaux-Arts mansions three or four stories high. The setting now is dominated by office blocks that have disturbed this scale; although if you place the memorial between yourself and Patterson House it is possible to visualize how it once was.

Walk now to the northeast side of the park to get a closer look at **Patterson House** (7). Designed by Stanford White (1853–1906) and completed in 1903, it represents a building designed more for entertainment than for residence. Note the marble ornamentation and the street number 15, set in a cartouche above the entrance like a ducal coat of arms. The house was actually built for Cissy Patter-

son's mother, Elinor, who had moved to Washington for the same reason that Mrs. Levi Leiter and Mrs. Tom Walsh (see page 71) were building winter palaces there. Unlike more exclusive Boston, New York, or Charleston, the booming capital welcomed any woman with money and talent who was intent on becoming an important society hostess.

Biographer Alice Hoge noted in her admirable *Cissy Patterson* (1966) that Elinor lived in an era in which women were denied legitimate outlets for their ambitions. Nonetheless, she succeeded in expressing hers by storming the social citadels of the Atlantic seaboard. Soon after its completion, Patterson House was the scene of balls and dinners attended by the beautiful people, notably the "Three Graces of Washington"—Alice Roosevelt, Countess Marguerite Cassini, and Cissy Patterson. (Evalyn Walsh McLean replaced Countess Cassini as the second Grace).

Shortly afterward, Cissy herself became a countess. At noon, on April 14, 1904, in the library of 15 Dupont Circle, in the presence of thirty-five people, including Pattersons, McCormicks, Theodore Roosevelt's daughter, Alice, and representatives of several embassies, Cissy became Countess Gizycka of the Austro-Hungarian Empire.

In 1920 Elinor suffered a serious heart attack, and returned to Chicago to live. It was Cissy's turn. Previously her mother's *palazzo* had depressed her, but she had decided not only to follow in her mother's footsteps as a big spender but to excel her. The house was kept full of guests simply because she found it depressing to live here alone. She employed a staff of ten, including a head butler, two chauffeurs, a seamstress, and a secretary, plus a squad of footmen in green livery.

In 1926 when she was living mostly in New York City, Cissy rented the house to Calvin Coolidge while the White House was undergoing repairs. Grace Coolidge found the living quarters cramped, expressing surprise that the public rooms were so grand in comparison. Nonetheless, she gave some of her most successful parties here. Her most noted guest was Charles Lindbergh, and during May 1927 the house was mobbed for three days as crowds chanted: "We want Lindy. We want Lindy." The bewildered hero appeared on the balcony from time to time, to acknowledge the tribute with a shy grin. He had electrified the world with his transatlantic flight. But Cissy wasn't impressed. She was glad to see the Coolidges go, she said, because the President fed his dogs scraps of meat on her dining-room rug.

After the death of her second husband, Elmer Schlesinger, in 1929, Cissy moved back into the house and 15 Dupont Circle entered its most lavish phase. Her parties outdazzled those of Evalyn Walsh McLean's in wit and sophistication. According to her friends, the one thing she had to have was a good argument, and she frequently invited guests who were certain to provide one. A typical guest list during the Thirties would include Ethel Barrymore, J. Edgar Hoover, Alger Hiss, John L. Lewis, Douglas MacArthur, and William Randolph Hearst. "Cissy," wrote Alice Hoge, from whose biography much of my account is derived, "provided glamor

and entertainment and not just another place for diplomats and politicians to do their business."

Throughout the years of the Great Depression, Cissy continued to entertain on a royal scale, cutting a striking figure in flamboyant outfits set off by diamonds or a magnificent black pearl necklace that had once belonged to Princess Irina Youssoupoff, wife of Rasputin's celebrated assassin. Sometimes Cissy didn't even bother to attend her own parties and ate by herself or stayed up late, drinking, writing, or reading. She had become an insomniac and occasionally would creep down to the kitchen and have a beer with the night watchman. Then she and her poodles would retire to bed, sometimes to the top floor where she had lived as a young debutante, and sometimes to her mother's room on the second floor, with the balcony looking onto Dupont Circle.

By 1943 Cissy, now sixty, spent less time in Washington, preferring to spend spring and early summer at Dower House, Maryland, a seventeenth-century mansion designed by Christopher Wren as a hunting lodge for Milords Baltimore. Midsummer was spent at her Sands Point estate, where the cool Long Island breezes made life more agreeable. Winter was spent in Sarasota, Florida, or Nassau. To an ailing Cissy, it must have seemed the end of an era, when despite a well-conducted campaign of protest in the *Times-Herald*, the District of Columbia went ahead and built the underpass for Connecticut Avenue under Dupont Circle. She died in 1948.

The funeral was held in the ballroom after a public viewing of the casket. Attracted by her notoriety, thousands filed through the great house and were awed by its opulence and objets d'art. This casual attitude concerning access by the public was not a good idea. So many small valuable objects vanished that day that security had to be doubled. Cissy's will left the house and its contents to the American Red Cross, which in 1949 auctioned her personal belongings and effects. Then in January of the following year, the house itself was purchased by the Washington Club. Fortunately, the sale included much of the fine furniture and tapestries.

Before continuing down New Hampshire Avenue to our next stop, the Whittemore House, glance at the shiplike mansion heading as it were into Dupont Circle at the right, on the corner of Massachusetts Avenue. This is the **Sulgrave Club***, formerly the residence of Herbert Wadsworth and his wife, Martha, the former Martha Blow, a St. Louis beauty. Wadsworth, an engineer, owned and managed agricultural properties in New York State's Genesee Valley. The architect is thought to have been Frederick Brooke. It was built between 1900 and 1901.

Proceed now to Whittemore House, a short walk up New Hampshire Avenue to Q Street.

Whittemore House

1526 New Hampshire Avenue, NW. A National Historic Landmark owned by the Women's National Democratic Club. Not open to the public.

Located on a triangular corner site bounded by New Hampshire Avenue and Q Street, **Whittemore House (8)**, sometimes called Weeks House, is distinctively different from the mansions we have seen, or will see on this walk. Designed by Washington architect Harvey Page (1859–1934), it is the most endearing of mansions, with a personality that has more in common with the shingle style of Newport, Rhode Island, than with the more pretentious Beaux-Arts style of Massachusetts Avenue. The irregularly shaped structure, tall massive chimneys, and the free-flowing capelike roof that covers a polygonal tower and eyelike dormer windows, give the house a fairytale monster look. Architect Phillip Johnson has described it as "an architectural masterpiece."

Whittemore House was built between 1892 and 1894 for Sarah Adams Whittemore, a descendant of President John Adams. After her death in 1907, the house was left to her son and daughter, who lived there at various times. Her son, Walter Dwight Wilcox, was a travel writer and photographer who between 1898 and 1909 published several travelogs on Canada and in 1924 a book on Cuba, where he owned a mahogany and cedar plantation.

From time to time, the house has had a number of well-known occupants. In 1903 Senator John F. Dryden of New Jersey rented the house. Dryden, one of the founders of the Prudential Insurance Company, was a Senator from 1902 to 1907, when he returned to the insurance business. Theodore P. Shonts, a wealthy railroad magnate, rented it during the winter of 1906–1907 for the debuts of his two daughters. Its best-known tenant was banker John C. Weeks (1860–1926) who rented the house from 1907 to 1911. While residing here he was Congressman from Massachusetts; he was a Senator from

Whittemore House (Women's National Democratic Club)

Woman's National Democratic Club

Paul HOGARTH: Weeks House

1913 to 1919 and Secretary of War under Harding and Coolidge, 1921–1925. Later Walter Wilcox and his family moved back into the house, living here until 1926. In 1927, after passing through the hands of various owners, it was finally bought by the Women's National Democratic Club.

Before turning left on Q Street, walk a few steps farther on New Hampshire to 18th Street to view the magnificent **Perry Belmont Mansion*** (now the Eastern Star Temple), 1618 New Hampshire Avenue. Not open to the public. Built in 1909 by diplomat Perry Belmont, the big-spending grandson of Commodore Matthew Calbraith Perry (1794–1858), it was one of America's most spectacular mansions and cost $1.5 million. During the Great Depression it was sold to the Order of the Eastern Star for $100,000. Unfortunately, this impressive house is seldom opened to public view.

The distinguished French architect Étienne Sansom collaborated with Horace Trumbauer to create a design in the Louis XIV style with materials and fixtures imported from Europe. The walls in the entrance hall are built of Normandy Caen stone. The state dining-room ceiling was brought from the Doge's Palace, Venice. Echoing the grandeur of Versailles are the carved marble doorways and window casings, its ornamental frescoes and friezes of carved oak, bronze chandeliers with crystal and amethyst drops, and gold leaf on the walls and ceilings. "Fit for a prince" aptly describes the fifty-four room Belmont mansion. It was here that the Prince of Wales, better known as the Duke of Windsor, later King Edward VIII of England, stayed for ten days in November 1919 while on an official visit to the United States. Distinguished heads of state used to stay here as they do today at Blair House (see page 19).

Now retrace your steps to Dupont Circle. Cross 19th Street and Connecticut Avenue to 20th and Q Streets and pass the **Colombian Embassy***, formerly the home of Francophile Thomas T. Gaff, inventor and sportsman. It was designed by deSibour, one of Washington's most prolific architects, in the manner of a sixteenth-century French château.

Continue up 20th past the Dupont Circle Metro Station to R Street. Turn left, then head up the north or right-hand side of the street. At 2131 R Street is the **Roosevelt House***. Franklin D. Roosevelt and his large brood lived here, 1917–1920, while he was Assistant Secretary of the Navy.

Next door at 2133 R Street is the delightful red-brick art nouveau studio house designed by Joseph Coerton Hornblower and Samuel Rush Marshall, and built in 1902 for Edward Lind Morse, artist, author, and son of Samuel Finley Breeze Morse (1791–1872), artist and inventor of the telegraph and the code named after him.

The **Morse House*** and Roosevelt House are private residences and are not open to the public.

Continue walking on R Street. Turn right on 22nd and cross Decatur Place to climb the picturesque Decatur Terrace steps and fountain, built 1911–1912 to link Decatur Place with the much higher S Street. You are now in the Kalorama district proper, originally part of a vast wooded estate. As the view from the top of the steps suggests, the estate looked out over the Potomac and the growing capital until the early years of the twentieth century. Then between 1900 and 1915, it was developed into an exclusive neighborhood of handsome, architect-designed mansions, inhabited by Congressmen, Senators, cabinet members, and Supreme Court justices before foreign governments began to buy them in the late 1920s and early 1930s.

Turn left on S Street. A short walk will bring you to our next stop, the Woodrow Wilson House.

Woodrow Wilson House

2340 S Street, NW. A National Historic Landmark owned by the National Trust for Historic Preservation. Telephone: (202)673-4034. Open February, Saturday and Sunday 12:00 NOON–4:00 P.M.; March through December, Tuesday through Friday 10:00 A.M.–2:00 P.M. Closed New Year's, Thanksgiving and Christmas. Admission (includes tour): Adults $2.50, senior citizens and children $1.00, special group rates available. Time: 30 minutes.

Woodrow Wilson (1856–1924) wanted to build his own house before he left the White House in 1921 but the former Princeton professor who put principles before men couldn't afford to do so. Instead, he did the next best thing and bought this handsome Georgian Revival house, now the **Woodrow Wilson House (9)**, designed by Waddy B. Wood and built in 1915 by businessman Henry Parker Fairbanks. Notice the Palladian-style windows on the second floor, a feature that may have played a part in helping Mrs. Wilson describe it as a "dignified house, fitted to the needs of a gentleman."

Wilson suffered a stroke in the autumn of 1919,

Woodrow Wilson House

although his wife, Edith, kept his disability a secret. Old and wasted, he lived out his remaining years in quiet seclusion here. He died three years after leaving office, on February 3, 1924. Edith Bolling Wilson occupied the house until her own death in 1961, and since then it has been preserved unchanged by the National Trust. Thus, the interior is just as it was when the Wilsons lived there.

The house provides many insights into the life and personality of this great American. On the second floor you will hear a record of his daughter singing that gives you the uncanny sensation of traveling back in time. Memorabilia, portrait paintings, and autographed photographs of persons involved with Wilson's administration line the walls. A long silk banner showing the Stars and Stripes flapping in the wind, the original Red Cross poster entitled *The Greatest Mother in the World*, and an empty brass shell case that held the first shot fired by American troops in World War I mingle with commemorative china and colonial furniture that was owned by the Bolling family of Virginia.

In the library, Wilson's favorite room, this ambience of the past is especially strong. I noticed a copy of H. G. Wells's *The Future in America* (1906) and remembered that the two men greatly admired one another. When war ended in 1918, the celebrated British writer urged Wilson to take a positive and constructive role at the Paris Peace Conference. Soon after the Armistice was signed on November 11, 1918, President Wilson sailed for Europe to help shape the peace. But he failed to check the newly victorious Allies that were intent on seeking revenge on Germany, thus creating the conditions that eventually led to World War II. Wilson believed that if a world organization could be established and given supervisory powers, future wars might be avoided. He never recovered from the rejection of his dream, the League of Nations.

Leaving the Wilson House, resume your stroll to the end of S Street. Now turn left on Massachusetts Avenue. On the corner is the former Hauge Mansion, now the Cameroon Embassy, our next stop.

Hauge Mansion (Cameroon Chancery)

2349 Massachusetts Avenue, NW. A National Historic Landmark owned by the Federal Republic of Cameroon. Not open to the public.

The châteauesque **Hauge Mansion (10)**, gracing the northwest corner of Massachusetts Avenue and 24th Street, was the scene of lavish parties in the 1920s. It was built in 1906–1907 by Mrs. Frederick Joy (the former Louise Grundy Todd of Louisville, Kentucky), a wealthy widow, for her husband, Norwegian diplomat Christian Hauge.

Hauge, who began his career, as an attaché in Paris and Berlin, came to Washington in 1901 as Secretary of the Legation for Sweden and Norway. After Norway became independent from Sweden in 1905, he was appointed Norway's first minister to the United States. Well-known socially in Washington and New York, and also in fashionable Bar Harbor, Maine, then the summer residence of the Sweden-Norway legation, the dashing blue-eyed

Hauge was an eligible bachelor. But not for long. He met Louise Todd at Bar Harbor and married her in 1904. Like most Washington hostesses, she quickly became the moving spirit in the relationship.

Their abode in the city did not fit his position as envoy extraordinary and minister plenipotentiary of the kingdom of Norway; nor was it spacious enough for the entertaining she had in mind.

In what was to have been a gesture of overkill, she hired George Oakley Totten, Jr., to design a mansion that would serve both as residence and legation. It was completed in June 1907. In November the Hauges left Washington for a three-month vacation in Europe. They visited Paris for the purpose of selecting furnishings and decorations that would grace their new home. Fate decreed otherwise. One month later, Mr. Hauge died unexpectedly on a snowshoeing trip near Oslo, Norway. A widow for the second time, Louise never remarried and the intended legation became her home until her death in 1927. The house then served as the Czechoslovakian Embassy from 1929 to 1969 and was vacant until sold in 1972 to the Federal Republic of Cameroon.

Ostentatiously Beaux-Arts in style, this limestone palace in the early sixteenth-century French manner is another example of Totten's eclecticism. Its richly Gothic elements include a conical tower capped by an elaborate weathervane finial. The gabled roof has two rows of dormer windows plus an intricate cast-iron railing with finials. I almost expected a beautiful damsel to rush to the second floor balcony to watch for the approach of her lover, a knight at arms on horseback.

While you are standing at the intersection of Massachusetts Avenue and S Street, glance at the Robert Emmet Park on your left. The statue (1917, Jerome Connor) was commissioned by Irish-Americans to commemorate Robert Emmet (1778–1803), the Irish patriot who led an abortive French-aided uprising and was captured and hanged by the British. It was placed here and dedicated on April 12, 1966, on the fiftieth anniversary of Irish independence.

This stage of the tour marks the western end of the mansions of Massachusetts Avenue built in the Beaux-Arts style. Now cross the avenue and proceed east one block to Sheridan Circle to view Alice Barney Studio House and the Sheridan Statue.

Emerson Emerson
(Le Hauge House)

Alice Barney Studio House

2306 Massachusetts Avenue, NW. A National Historic Landmark owned by the Smithsonian Institution. Telephone: (202)357-3111. Open from October through May. Free tours (by appointment only). Time: 45 minutes.

Alice Pike Barney (c. 1857–1931) was one of those grandes dames of art whose doings were always the life of every party and the talk of the town. She was a strikingly handsome woman, wealthy and incredibly energetic. She produced several hundred paintings of questionable quality and authored at least fifty plays. Daring in her personal life, she was regarded by many as a priestess of high fashion. She was, in fact, a free woman, secure enough to question the traditions of the socially oriented world from which she sprang, using Art with a capital *A* as the means of escape from the grinding round of hostessing for a more-than-dull railroad-car heir husband, Albert Clifford Barney of Dayton, Ohio.

His death in 1902 gave her the chance to establish the Spanish mission-style **Studio House (11)** as both workshop and salon, which, she hoped, would make Washington a cultural center comparable to her beloved Paris. Designed with the help of Waddy B. Wood and completed in 1903, Studio House was where it was all at until 1925. Here, she entertained celebrities by the carriageload, from Theodore Roosevelt and Taft to Caruso and the dancers Anna Pavlova and Ruth St. Denis.

The fantasies of the interior are said to defy any attempt at description. Sarah Booth Conroy in a *Washington Post* article had a good try, however, when she wrote of "balconies, stages, alcoves, carved columns, languorous banquettes, handmade tile floors, huge-hewn beamed ceilings, peep holes, and massive fireplaces and a good many things hard to name." "All of these," she added, "were dressed with tapestries, wallpaper, fabric wall coverings, wall murals, velvet cornices, neo-medieval furniture, gilded mottoes, gilded mirrors, castle-sized chandeliers, brocade hangings, piles of pillows, a zoo of animal skins, and a museum of decorative objects."

As you return to our starting point, the Bison Bridge, have a glance at the vigorous **Sheridan Statue** (1908, Gutzon Borglum, the sculptor of Mt. Rushmore). Mrs. Sheridan liked it so much that she built 2211 Massachusetts Avenue to be close to the memory of her warrior husband, General Phillip Henry Sheridan (1831–1888), Civil War hero and Indian fighter.

We have now completed our tour of the mansions of Massachusetts Avenue.

Alice Barney Studio House

Paul Hogarth
Sheridan Statue & Studio House...

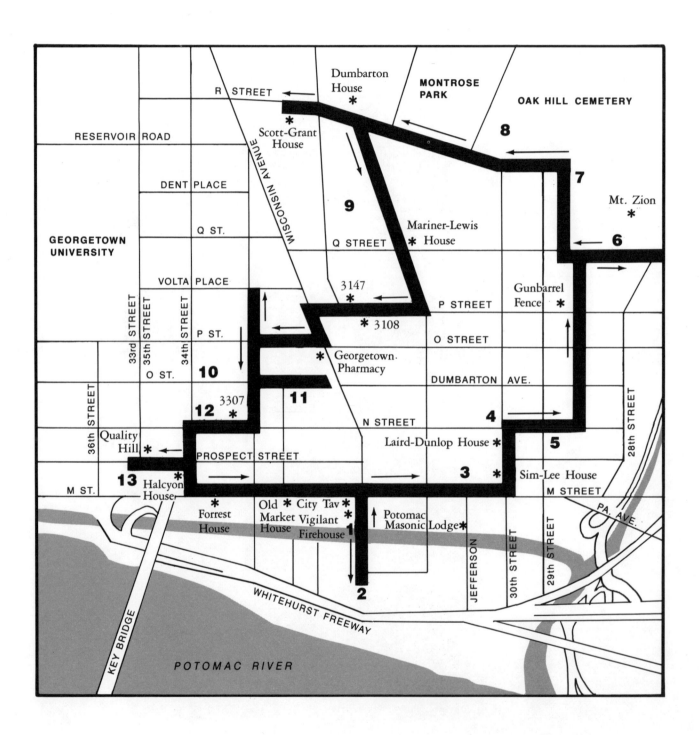

R STREET

Dumbarton House *

MONTROSE PARK

OAK HILL CEMETERY

Scott-Grant House *

8

RESERVOIR ROAD

DENT PLACE

7

Mt. Zion *

Q ST.

9

Mariner-Lewis * House

6

GEORGETOWN UNIVERSITY

WISCONSIN AVENUE

Q STREET

VOLTA PLACE

3147 *

P STREET

Gunbarrel Fence *

33rd STREET

35th STREET

34th STREET

P ST.

* 3108

O STREET

10

O ST.

* Georgetown Pharmacy

DUMBARTON AVE.

36th STREET

3307 *

11

N STREET

4

12

28th STREET

Quality Hill *

PROSPECT STREET

Laird-Dunlop House *

5

13 Halcyon House *

3 *

Sim-Lee House

M ST.

Forrest House *

Old Market House *

City Tav *

Vigilant Firehouse *

Potomac Masonic Lodge *

M STREET

PA. AVE.

JEFFERSON

30th STREET

29th STREET

1

2

WHITEHURST FREEWAY

KEY BRIDGE

POTOMAC RIVER

Georgetown

Distance: 4 miles. Time: 3 hours. Metrobus: any 30 (to 31st and M Streets, NW). Parking: strictly limited on streets; commercial lots below M Street and by Old Stone House. Restaurants: along M Street and Wisconsin Avenue there are many good restaurants and light-food establishments, ranging from expensive to inexpensive.

Georgetown, the residential district for proper Washingtonians, or cliff dwellers, began in 1751 as a bustling tobacco port. It was named in honor of George II, the reigning king of England. Its location below the Great Falls of the Potomac made it a natural port for the inland plantations of the Maryland piedmont. The first settlers were Scots merchants who exported tobacco, furs, and lumber to the Old World and imported fine furniture, "furbelows," and wines for affluent colonials. By the time the Federal City was established in 1800, Georgetown was an official port of entry, thriving on its river—and from 1830—canal-born commerce.

Georgetown also prospered from being the only settled community for miles, able to accommodate the incoming officials and their families, and hangers-on while Washington suffered the agonies of construction. Then, when railroads replaced canals as a more flexible means of transport, Georgetown saw the end of its days as a viable commercial center. The Potomac silted up, and the waterfront, which was industrial, was run-down. By 1871 Georgetown had become a middle-class neighborhood.

It was an end, but it also was a beginning. Some restoration had taken place by World War I and many of the fine old houses had been restored by the end of the 1920s. But after 1934, during Roosevelt's New Deal, growing numbers of civil servants led by a social and political elite found Georgetown a congenial and inexpensive place in which to live. They began restoration of the many old houses that had fallen into disrepair, a process that continued after World War II.

Today residents of Georgetown, a stylish mixture of trendily chic and the severely diffident, take pride in living in an historic neighborhood of venerable Federal houses and sleepy, tree-shaded streets. The Old Georgetown Act, which defined the Historic District, requires that building and demolition grants be submitted to the Commission of Fine Arts. In 1967 Georgetown was designated a National Historic District.

So here you can see much that delights the eye. Streets are narrow and are lined with gnarled old trees. The difference in ambience changes from street to street. Georgetown Heights, far above the Potomac, boasts large estates from the eighteenth and early nineteenth centuries, an incredible few with their grounds intact, that mingle with more modest houses of later vintages. Georgetown's lower reaches are less residential, giving one the sense of living in a city.

Begin your tour at the obelisk commemorating the completion of the Chesapeake and Ohio canal (now a National Historic Park), on Wisconsin Avenue, a block below M Street.

Chesapeake and Ohio Canal National Historic Park

Open daily from dawn till dusk. Telephone: (202)299-3613 for information, (202)299-2026 for barge trip schedules.

The history of the **Chesapeake and Ohio Canal (1)** goes back to the middle of the eighteenth century when a long-talked-about project to tap the trade of the Ohio Valley prompted local merchants to back George Washington's idea of a water route connecting the Atlantic Ocean and the Ohio River (and the Mississippi) via the Potomac Valley. As an assistant on survey expeditions sent out in 1748 and 1753, Washington had more knowledge of, and contact with, the region than most men at the time. Wash-

Chesapeake and Ohio Canal National Historic Park

ington's Potomac Company made five "skirting canals" on the Virginia side of the river.

The small granite obelisk behind the iron fence commemorates the completion of the canal as far as Cumberland. President John Quincy Adams turned the first spade of earth on July 4, 1828. One year later more than three thousand men, including a large contingent of Irish navvies fresh from their railroad-building triumphs in England, were at work. But by the time the canal reached Cumberland in 1850, the Baltimore and Ohio Railroad had already proved that freight could be moved much faster and more cheaply than barges drawn by mules. Therefore, the last hundred miles, originally planned to reach Pittsburgh, were never built. This historic marker was discovered in an old Georgetown mill and erected here in 1900.

While the canal didn't bring any spectacular measure of economic prosperity, it provided a leisurely means of shipping coal, flour, grain, and lumber to Washington. In the early summer of 1889 a huge flood devastated banks, bridges, and locks and left them in ruins. The canal was rebuilt and used until 1924, when another great flood struck, ending all commercial usage. By 1954 plans had been made to fill in the canal and build a highway on its right of way. At this point, the old Chesapeake and Ohio found a champion in William Orville Douglas, Supreme Court Justice and conservationist-extraordinary. Douglas's incredible crusade, which culminated in a much-publicized eight-day hike from Cumberland to Georgetown along the old towpath, focused attention on the historic canal and helped defeat the highway project. By 1960 the project was abandoned and the canal designated a national monument. Furthermore Congress passed additional legislation in 1971, creating the Chesapeake and Ohio Canal Historical Park. Today the restored canal provides a welcome parklike retreat for joggers, weekend strollers, cross-country hikers, bird-watchers, and bicyclists.

Stone bridges arched the canal where it cut across streets. These were built at 29th, 30th, Thomas Jefferson, and 31st Streets. All these were replaced by iron structures after the Civil War. The one you are looking at, built about 1830, is the only surviving example of the original stone type. Before crossing the bridge, give a glance behind you at the **Vigilant Firehouse***, the oldest existing firehouse in the District of Columbia, built for the Vigilant Fire Company in 1844. Set in the wall at the right

of the entrance is a sad memento of its history, a burial plaque mourning the demise of "Bush, the old fire dog. Died of Poison, July 5, R.I.P." Bush, a faithful collie who went along to every fire atop the engine, was the firefighters' mascot.

Old Dodge Warehouses

1000–1006 Wisconsin Avenue, NW. A National Historic Landmark. Not open to the public.

Continue down Wisconsin one block. At the corner of K and Wisconsin, almost under the Whitehurst Freeway, are the **Old Dodge Warehouses (2)**, the last surviving examples of the many warehouses that once lined the Georgetown waterfront. Between 1813 and 1857 traders passed through these battered doors to buy Cuban molasses, Santo Domingo coffee, and Havana "seegars." Francis Dodge, who arrived in Georgetown as an industrious Yankee lad of eighteen from Newburyport, Massachusetts, soon made a fortune as a trader and merchant in West Indies goods. His sons, however, were not as lucky. After their father's death, they continued his trade for six years but lost all in the Panic of 1857. Historians say that this type of warehouse was used in Holland and England from the Middle Ages to the beginning of the nineteenth century. The red-brick walls on stone foundations with cast-iron, starshaped wall anchors are characteristic features.

Now cross the street and walk back up Wisconsin. Turn right before Grace Episcopal Church on South Street. Turn left again on 31st Street and walk up to the bridge. Cross the bridge and turn right onto the brick-walkway to Thomas Jefferson Street. On your immediate left is the former **Potomac Masonic Lodge*** (1058 Jefferson Street), built in 1810. Members of this lodge were present at the laying of the Capitol's cornerstone in 1793.

Proceed one block north up Thomas Jefferson to M Street.

Old Dodge Warehouses

Old Stone House

3051 M Street, NW. A National Historic Landmark owned and administered by the National Park Service. Telephone: (202)426-6851. Open daily 9:30 A.M.–5:00 P.M. Free. Group and school tours by appointment. Time: 15–20 minutes.

Between 30th and 31st Streets on the north side of M is the **Old Stone House (3)**, believed to be the oldest surviving pre-Revolutionary building in the District of Columbia. Built in 1765 by Christopher Lehman (or Layman), the house was inhabited by one family after another as a home and a workshop. Lehman, a cabinetmaker by trade who came to Georgetown from Pennsylvania, had his shop on the ground floor. Some of his tools were among the twenty cases of artifacts found by archeologists during restoration in 1956.

The house was acquired in 1767 by Cassandra Chew, who added the north wing sometime during the 1770s. Mrs. Chew, a widow, lived here briefly with her two daughters, Mary and Harriet. Other occupants included a clockmaker, a tailor, and gunsmith Reuben Daw. The Chew family eventually moved to a larger house but the Old Stone House remained in the Chew family until the early nineteenth century, when the eldest daughter, Mary, by that time a widow, lived there with her two sons and four daughters.

The simple old house, reminiscent of the

Old Stone House

fieldstone farmhouses of eastern Pennsylvania, was once thought to be the famous Fountain Inn, run by John Suter, where L'Enfant had his office while surveying the new capital. It has since been proved that the house was not Suter's Tavern.

Five of the rooms are furnished as they would have been during the late eighteenth century. The kitchen and the workshop on the ground floor provided the busiest scenes of everyday life. The paneled dining room, a bedroom, and a parlor on the floor above are where the family lived after the shop closed for the day.

At the corner of 30th and M is the **Thomas Sim Lee House***. Built in the 1790s, it was for many years the home of Thomas Lee, friend of Washington and ardent revolutionary. He was a Maryland delegate to the Continental Congress in 1783 and 1784, and a member of the state convention that ratified the Constitution. A pillar of the Federal party, he was twice Governor of Maryland. One should add that the house was saved from demolition in 1951 through the efforts of Dorothea de Schweinitz, who helped form Historic Georgetown, Inc., which purchased and restored the Thomas Sim Lee House and adjacent buildings.

Leave M Street by 30th Street and walk up one block to N. Turn left on N. A short stroll up N Street quickly imparts the distinctive flavor created

Beall House

by the fine Federal houses that line this oldest of Washington's residential streets. At 3014 is the **Laird-Dunlop House***, built about 1799 by John Laird, the prosperous owner of one of Georgetown's great tobacco warehouses. The house has been attributed to both Thornton and Hadfield. But in all probability its builder may have used a pattern book. Later owners included Judge Dunlop, Chief Justice of the Supreme Court until removed as a Confederate sympathizer by Lincoln; and from 1915–1926 by Robert Todd Lincoln, eldest son of the President, one time Secretary of War, Ambassador to England, and president of the Pullman Company.

Now turn to view the handsome **Beall House** (4) sitting up on high at 3017. Thomas, grandson of Ninian Beall, the best known of the original owners of the land that is now Washington, was the mayor of Georgetown who met with George Washington in 1791 to discuss Georgetown's incorporation with the District of Columbia. The house was built *c.* 1794 and has had many distinguished and famous residents since, among them Newton D. Baker (1871–1936), Secretary of War in Wilson's cabinet, who is believed to have started the fashion for living in Georgetown. Jacqueline Kennedy lived in the house for a year before she fled the public gaze to the anonymity of a Manhattan apartment on Fifth Ave-

Decatur House (Morsell House)

nue. An interesting feature of the three-story house is the captain's walk above the third floor. In the days of sailing ships, merchants and traders used such vantage points atop their houses to look down on the Potomac to see if their vessels were approaching Georgetown. The great magnolia trees that screen the facade were planted the year the house was built and bloom magnificently each April through June.

From the Beall House continue east down N Street to 29th Street. Between 29th and 28th at 2812 is the **Decatur House (5)** or Morsell House. This superb Federal townhouse, with its elegant doorcase, was built in 1816 by architect-builder John Stull Williams. Susan Decatur is said to have lived here after leaving the mansion on Lafayette Square following her husband's tragic death (see page 21). For many years it was the home of Samuel Humphries, chief naval constructor, U.S. Navy.

Continue to the end of the block to 28th Street. The little frame house at 2804 has a more modest claim to fame. It was, from 1955 to 1958, the home of movie actress Myrna Loy and her husband Howland Sargeant, former Assistant Secretary of State under Eisenhower.

Turn left and walk up 28th Street. At the northwest corner of 28th and P is the **Gunbarrel Fence***, Georgetown curiosity and guardian of the Federal

Dumbarton House (National Society of Colonial Dames)

houses at 2803 to 2811 P Street, some of which have been occupied by distinguished families over the years. For example, Dean Acheson who lived at 2805. The builder was the thrifty gunsmith Reuben Daw, who purchased a consignment of surplus, outdated muskets at a Navy Yard auction. By removing the stocks and adding spikes or plates at the end of the barrels, he made a unique fence for his houses.

Continue up 28th Street and turn right on Q. Between 28th and 27th Streets is our next stop, Dumbarton House.

Dumbarton House

2715 Q Street, NW. A National Historic Landmark owned and administered by the National Society of Colonial Dames of America as its national headquarters. Telephone: (202)337-2288. Open Monday through Saturday 9:00 A.M.–12:00 NOON. Closed Sunday and July through August. Free. Time: 30 minutes.

Dumbarton House (6), called Bellevue before its purchase by the Colonial Dames in 1928, was one of the first great houses to be built on the heights above the Potomac. Surrounded by great woods and rolling fields, such estates were largely self-supporting, with their own farms. The site itself was originally owned by Ninian Beall and was part of his 795-acre tract called the Rock of Dumbarton after the well-known Scots landmark north of the Clyde.

The house was built by Samuel Jackson about 1799–1800; its original architect is unknown, although Latrobe designed additions and embellishments. Following Jackson there were three changes of ownership before Gabriel Duval, comptroller of currency, sold the house in 1805 to Joseph Nourse, registrar of the Treasury. As the Federal city emerged, such properties changed hands frequently. The Nourse family, however, lived in the house for seven years and were its first real residents. During their stay, the young Robert Mills, architect of the Washington Monument, was a paying guest.

In 1813 the house was purchased by Charles Carroll, the same Charles Carroll who gave shelter to Dolley Madison in her hour of need after the British invaded the capital and burned the White House (see page 13). When Charles acquired the property he engaged Latrobe to design an entrance portico and other improvements, although Nourse had also sought his advice concerning changes.

From 1820 until the end of the nineteenth century, Bellevue was owned by various prominent personages. But as each family lived here for comparatively few years, the house has not been restored as the home of a single famous person but as an outstanding example of an early Federal mansion embellished with fine furniture, china, and memorabilia that once belonged to the notable families of the day. With a view overlooking Rock Creek Park to the rear, Dumbarton House is a peaceful, almost bucolic, enclave in today's busy Georgetown.

On leaving Dumbarton House, turn left and walk to Mills Road. Turn left again and you will see **Mount Zion Cemetery***. Dating back to 1808, this forgotten graveyard was originally bound by Rock Creek Park. Although saved by its designation as a National Historic Landmark, the cemetery awaits restoration as a reminder of the contribution of the black community to Georgetown's history. Meanwhile, to quote Ira Glackens:

Under toppled stones we lie,
Broken bottles, rusty tins—
Can this be the place from where
The Preacher told us, "Life begins?"

Retrace your steps to Dumbarton House and continue to 28th Street. Turn left on 28th. At the northeast corner of 28th and Q look out for a small stone marker erected by the Colonial Dames to mark the "Beginning of Evermay," your next stop.

Evermay

1623 28th Street, NW. A National Historic Landmark owned by Mrs. Peter Belin. Not open to the public.

Set well back from 28th Street behind a high ivy-clad wall, this handsome Federal house is another survivor of Old Georgetown. Everymay (7) was built for Samuel Davidson between 1801 and 1810 from plans by Nicholas King. Davidson, a bachelor, a Scotsman from Annapolis, and a wealthy merchant-*cum*-realtor drawn to the area by the prospects of the new Federal City, never lived here, but spent most of his time at the Union Tavern (a famous local hostelry) where he lodged and closed his deals. Edward, a faithful retainer, armed with cudgel, tomahawk, cutlass, gun, and blunderbuss, kept an eye on things.

King, a Yorkshireman who emigrated to America in 1794, worked with the district surveyor's office and was also the first librarian of Washington's first library. Although he was trained as an architect in England, Everymay was his only known venture into architecture. In addition to his design for the house, King also designed the original garden, all for a fee of $45.00. But then the total cost of building the entire house was only $897.40!

The building standing before us is the result of

Evermay

extensive restoration. The house had lost its Federal character in 1877 when it was remodeled in the Victorian style of the day. Sometime after 1923, however, it was stripped of Victoriana by a new owner, Lamont Belin, former U.S. Ambassador to Poland. Belin not only restored the house to its original state but also added the service wing and formal gardens.

Continue up R Street to 30th along the tall elaborate cast-iron fence of Oak Hill Cemetery. This brings us to the cemetery's main entrance gate.

Oak Hill Cemetery

R Street at 30th Street, NW. A National Historic Landmark owned by the Oak Hill Cemetery Company. Telephone: (202)337-2835. Open Monday through Friday 9:00 A.M.– 5:00 P.M. Closed Saturday and Sunday. Free. Time: 15 minutes; more if you are a graveyard buff.

It was early summer when I made my first visit to **Oak Hill Cemetery (8)** at the top of the hill above

Georgetown. Its 25 acres, which comprise ravines and plateaus with rocky banks along Rock Creek Park, reminded me of an Italian cemetery, although it is different in the size of its tombs and mausoleums, which are set along winding paths pleasantly shaded by a grove of great oak trees for which the cemetery was named.

Chartered by Congress in 1849, the land was purchased by W. W. Corcoran, who commissioned George de la Roche (1791–1861) to lay out the cemetery as a landscaped park with curving drives and terraces and an Italianate gatekeeper's house. Oak Hill is crowded with fascinating monuments, mausoleums, and grave-markers. Their common trait is the language of symbolism—the broken-column shaft, the inverted torch, the draped urn, and the angel symbolizing life after death in Kingdom Come. Just inside the entrance gate is the stately monument to John Howard Payne (1791–1852), author of "Home Sweet Home." Corcoran, an intimate friend, had the body exhumed and brought to the cemetery from Tunis where Payne had died after serving as U.S. Consul.

Beside the graves of families closely associated with Georgetown—Beall, Linthicum, Marbury, Thomas, and others—lie the remains of many persons celebrated and respected in their time, some of whom we will encounter again on our walks. Among them are Edwin McMasters Stanton (1814–1869), Secretary of War under Lincoln, (see page 34); James G. Blaine (see page 74); Alexander de Bodisco, the celebrated Russian diplomat, about whom you will be reading more on page 104, buried here in 1854; also Peggy O'Neale Eaton, whose marriage to Andrew Jackson's Secretary of War split the cabinet; Confederate General Jesse Lee Reno, who fell at the Battle of South Mountain, 1862; and last, but certainly not least, the worthy Corcoran himself. At the eastern end of the cemetery is the impressive monument to John Peter Van Ness and other Van Ness family members, designed by George Hadfield and modeled after the Temple of Vesta.

Oak Hill Cemetery Chapel itself, built in 1850 of Potomac stone, is well worth a visit because it is the only example of Renwick's Gothic Revival style in the District of Columbia. Its simple and restrained design represents a contrast to this architect's Smithsonian "castle" on the Mall and St. Patrick's Cathedral in New York City. Death—to paraphrase Senator Samuel Hoar of Massachusetts—surely can hold no terror amidst such congenial surroundings.

Continue on R Street past Montrose Park to the romantically shaded lane that appropriately enough since 1900 has been officially christened Lover's Lane. This leafy lane is the eastern boundary of **Dumbarton Oaks Research Library and Collection***, 1703 32nd Street, NW, another estate once part of Ninian Beall's patent. The house was built about 1801 but its most recent owners, Mr. and Mrs. Robert Woods Bliss, made extensive alterations and additions after 1920. In 1940 they gave the property to Harvard, which uses it as a study and research center. It was here in 1944 that the Dumbarton Oaks Conference that led to the drafting of the United Nations Charter was held. The art collections are housed in various wings and include Greek and Roman sculpture and Byzantine art. The Museum of Pre-Columbian Art, designed by Phillip Johnson and built in 1963, houses an outstanding collection of early South and Central American art. Open Tuesday through Sunday 2:00–5:00 P.M. Closed holidays.

Leaving Dumbarton Oaks, cross 32nd Street on R. At 3238 R Street, is the **Scott-Grant House***, an imposing Victorian edifice built in 1858. As Grant spent only a summer here, it really should be called the Scott-Halleck House. For the duration of the Civil War, General Henry Wager Halleck (who from 1862 replaced McClellan as commander-in-chief of the Union army) rented what was the residence of A. V. Scott of Alabama. In her book, *A Walk in Georgetown* (1966), Mary Mitchell informs us that Halleck was an unpopular tenant. A detail of enlisted men was quartered to the rear of the house, and their bugles blowing reveille and taps day and night, as well as their drilling up and down R Street, exasperated the neighbors. Many were Southern sympathizers and Halleck's presence there added insult to injury.

Retrace your steps and turn right on 31st Street. At the end of the block, on the left-hand corner of 31st and Q, is the fascinating **Mariner-Lewis House*** at 3099 Q Street, another example of the baronial style favored by Victorian businessmen anxious to emblematize their newly acquired fortunes.

On your way down 31st Street look out for the entrance gates on the west (or right-hand) side of the street. These are the gates of **Tudor Place (9)** at 1644 31st Street. As the house is a private residence, you cannot enter, nor, in fact, can you see it from this angle. Proceed to the intersection of 31st

Oak Hill Cemetery

and Q. Turn right and walk a few steps to obtain the best possible view of this beautiful mansion, which was for so many years the center of Washington society. Here the great and distinguished were feted and entertained; Lafayette was a visitor as was the defeated Confederate general, Robert E. Lee.

Tudor Place was originally built about 1797 by the wealthy tobacco merchant Francis Lowndes. He completed the east and west wings, then changed his mind and sold the partially completed house to Thomas Peter and his wife, Martha, the grand-daughter of Martha Washington. William Thornton, an intimate friend of the Peters, designed the main part of the house, making minor changes to the wings and joining them together with a high central block with a projecting semicircular south porch. Peter completed the mansion about 1815.

Since Tudor Place is not open to the public, it might be appropriate here to give you not an outline of its contents but a biographical account of Thornton, with whom I have dealt somewhat unkindly on previous walks (see pages 15 and 53).

Born of English Quaker parents in the Virgin Islands, Thornton was sent as a boy of five to live with indulgent aunts on the family estate near Lancaster, England, and receive his education. He took a doctor's degree in medicine at Aberdeen University in 1784. Two years later, he was back in the West Indies. But, after the pleasures of Europe, which included meeting Franklin and Hercshel in London, life on the plantation must have seemed dull. He embarked for the United States in October 1786, having decided that America might be more receptive to his ideals and ambitions.

Once there he lost no time in being involved with events *and* the right people. He was in Philadelphia in 1787 when the Constitutional Congress was assembled and became a friend of Madison. Remarkably, he proposed the abolition of slavery and the establishment of a free American state in Puerto Rico, but Madison and his friends succeeded in cooling the ardor of his unease with the paradox of owning slaves while advocating their freedom. He designed Library Hall, became a member of the Franklin set, and married Anna Maria Brodeau, daughter of a well-known Quaker family and a pupil of Gilbert Stuart, who acted as her husband's "draft-person," making detailed drawings from his rough notes and sketches. This proved to be a vital collaboration. Thornton won the competition for the design of the new Capitol.

101

Tudor Place

He then moved to Washington, where he was appointed one of the district commissioners, working with Washington and L'Enfant on the planning of the new city. This enabled him to play an influential role in the design and construction of all new buildings. In 1802 he was made superintendent of the Patent Office and became involved with an incredible range of interests, including a phonetic alphabet, a talking machine, and artifical ice.

Thornton had great taste. Many of his houses have disappeared, but what remains, notably Tudor Place and The Octagon (see Walk One) establish him as a skillful practitioner of the Federal style.

Now continue down 31st Street and turn right on P Street. At 3108 lived George Henry Thomas (1816–1870), the short-lived but celebrated Union general who, during the Chattanooga campaign of 1863, saved the Union army from defeat and was thus nicknamed the "Rock of Chickamauga." The mansard-roofed yellow Victorian house at 3147, on the opposite side of the street, once belonged to the English novelist Elinor Glyn (1864–1943), famous for her highly romantic tales with luxurious settings and improbable plots. Georgetown had always appealed greatly to her, with its gracious old houses, its cosmopolitan atmosphere, and its diplomatic society. She decided to make her home here and spent the autumn and winter of 1928–1929 redecorating the house. But shortly before she moved in, she paid a visit to England, intending to stay a few weeks with friends and family. In fact, she remained in England for the rest of her life.

Proceed to the intersection of P Street and Wisconsin Avenue. Cross Wisconsin and continue on P to 33rd Street. Turn right and walk up 33rd past 1524, the 'Old White Horse Tavern*' a picturesque building erected about 1812 although it was never as the marker states, a tavern.

Now retrace your steps to 33rd and contine to O Street. Turn right and look for our next stop, the Bodisco House.

Bodisco House

103

Bodisco House

3322 O Street, NW. A National Historic Landmark. Private residence. Not open to the public.

On the south side of O Street is the massive **Bodisco House (10)**, built in 1815 by Clement Smith of the Farmers' and Mechanics' Bank of Georgetown.

Later it became the Russian legation and here, at a fabulous Christmas party in 1838, sixty-two-year-old Baron Alexander de Bodisco, Russian minister to the United States, met his future wife, sixteen-year-old Harriet Brooke Williams. That night, the wealthy, worldly wise diplomat, fell in love with the tall beautiful daughter of a minor government official. It was the beginning of a romance that became so absorbing a topic of conversation that the Panic of 1837–1838 was almost forgotten.

Precocious Harriet became as deeply attached to her young-at-heart lover as he was to her. It was not smooth sailing at first, however. Harriet's family was strongly opposed to the marriage. She told the baron that her grandmother and everybody else thought he was much too old, much too stout, and much too ugly. The baron's reply was that they might find someone younger and perhaps better-looking, but no one who would love her as much and give her the security she wanted. A settlement was made and Harriet willingly accepted the baron, dyed hair, whiskers, mustache, and all.

They were married in April 1840 at the home of the bride's mother. Bodisco, dressed in blue-and-silver court uniform, pulled out all the stops. The bride, looking "unsurpassingly beautiful, distinguished by a charming ease, simplicity and gentleness," was given away by Senator Henry Clay, backed up by a phalanx of groomsmen that included Senator (later President) Buchanan, the eccentric Henry Stephen Fox, British Minister; Baron Saruyse, Austrian Minister, and Martin Van Buren, Jr., the son of the President. Fourteen-year-old Jessie Benton, who was also to marry a much older man, John "Pathfinder" Freemont, was one of a bevy of teenage bridesmaids.

At the brilliant reception that followed at Bodisco House, the bride and the groom received a crowd of even more distinguished guests, including President Van Buren and Daniel Webster. Bodisco's wealth allowed him to give his young wife everything she could possibly wish for, and the house became fa-

mous for the lavish magnificence of its entertaining. Long after the baron's death in 1854, Washington society still marveled at the enduring success of what had seemed so unsuitable a marriage.

Retrace your steps on O and cross 33rd and Potomac to Old St. John's Episcopal Church.

Old St. John's Church

3240 O Street, NW. Individual Landmark, Category III, Georgetown Historic District. Telephone: (202)338-1796. Services: first Sunday in June to first Sunday in September, 8:00 A.M. and 10:00 A.M.; September through May, 8:00 A.M., 9:00 A.M., 11:00 A.M. Visitors welcome. Time: 15 minutes.

At the corner of O and Potomac Streets is **Old St. John's Church (11)**, third-oldest Episcopalian church in the District of Columbia, preceded only by St. Paul's, Rock Creek; and Christ Church, Capitol Hill. Lawyer Francis Scott Key (1779–1843), the author of "The Star-Spangled Banner," was a vestryman here for many years and used to walk from the Key family house at 35th and M Streets to attend to his duties.

And these were very demanding. No church suffered such ups and downs in its endeavors to establish itself. The majority of Georgetown's merchants at this time were Scots and Presbyterian. On three occasions "its fate," to quote Mary Mitchell again, "hung by a hair." The first was in 1803, when after construction of the church had gone on since 1796, with walls only half completed, the vestry ran out of money. Someone came to the rescue, for the church was finished "in good taste" by 1806 and consecrated by Reverend Thomas J. Claggert, whose wife, remarkably enough, was Mary Mackall Gantt, a descendant of John Gantt, Duke of Lancaster, the son of Edward III, King of England and father of Henry IV!

Until St. John's Church at 16th and H Streets opened in 1816, Christ Church on Capitol Hill was the only other Episcopalian church within Washington's city limits. Consequently, St. John's, Georgetown, was crowded with prominent Washingtonians. Seats became so scarce that pews were fitted into the gallery. During Sunday service, carriages and liveried servants lined the streets outside. By the end of the 1820s, however, this mass influx

Old St. John's Church

became a thing of the past as Latrobe's St. John's (see page 22) was enlarged. By 1831, with so many of its pew rentals canceled, a second crisis finally closed the church down and the building was sold for taxes. Old St. John's, nicknamed "Swallow Barn," was rented to a sculptor for a studio. But Georgetown Episcopalians were, and still are, a determined lot. Seven years later, a sewing circle of young ladies had raised enough money to buy the church back.

The Civil War was the cause of another crisis. The simple neoclassical interior of 1844 was now too small, but plans to enlarge it were held up by lack of funds. Governor Henry D. Cooke came forward as the patron of change, and the interior was stripped and remodeled in the Victorian style as was the exterior in 1870. But the final chapter of the metamorphosis of Old St. John's was yet to come. In 1924, while rummaging around in the steeple, the incumbent rector discovered the original "pepperpot" belfry still in position. The Victorian wooden structure was forthwith removed and the facade restored to its former glory as a Federal edifice.

Before you continue the tour, glance at the Georgetown Pharmacy, (established 1883) on the corner of O and Wisconsin. For many years, the drugstore was the domain of "Doc" Darlinsky, its Norman Rockwellian proprietor, who entertained the luminaries of the press and the judiciary with coffee and bagels while holding forth on the state of nations.

Cox's Row

Turn left on Potomac Street and walk south to N Street. Turn right on N. At 3307 is the house that Senator John Fitzgerald Kennedy bought for Jacqueline after their daughter Caroline's birth in 1957. Next move, the White House. At the northeast corner of 34th and N Streets, stretching for almost half a block down to 33rd Street is **Cox's Row (12)**.

Colonel John Cox, a prosperous merchant, built these Federal townhouses in 1817, and they remain among the finest of Georgetown's large, handsome houses, distinguished by their ivy-clad facades, paneled swags, and venerable shutters.

Colonel Cox was mayor of Georgetown at the time of Lafayette's official visit in 1824. Vacant at

Cox's Row

the time, 3337 was quickly furnished for the stay of the aged hero. Even the edges of the floors were decorated by floral garlands drawn in colored chalks by schoolgirls. At a famous dinner here, hosted by Mayor Cox's eldest daughter, Lafayette was plentifully served with his favorite American game dish—the reed bird, or bobolink, of the southern marshes—at the time the succulent equivalent of the European blackbird or thrush.

Cox's former home at 3339 was later the residence

Cox's Row, N Street Georgetown

of Commodore Charles Morris, a naval hero of the Tripolitan War of 1801–1805. During the War of 1812 he served as an executive officer of the *Constitution* ("Old Ironsides") under Captain Isaac Hull.

Continue south down 34th to Prospect Street. Turn right on Prospect. At the northeast corner of 35th and Prospect is **Quality Hill***, built in 1797–1798 by John Thomson Mason, nephew of George Mason (1725–1792), the Revolutionary statesman who wrote the Virginia Bill of Rights.

His nephew, John Thomson Mason, was a lawyer, one of a group of Virginian gentry drawn from the counties to Georgetown by the activity generated by the rapidly growing capital. At this time, Quality Hill was the scene of much socializing. Some of the guests were leaders of the nation, including the great Jefferson himself who, on one occasion, according to Mason, arrived so plainly dressed that a servant refused to admit him. The house is said to have been named Quality Hill by a subsequent owner, Dr. Charles Worthington, an austere but humane Federalist who practiced medicine in Georgetown for more than half a century.

Continue on Prospect. Here more prosperous citizens built substantial residences where they could enjoy the commanding view of the Potomac and the wooded vistas beyond. At 3508 is one such residence, **Prospect House** (13), a free-standing Federal mansion built in 1788 by General James Maccubbin Lingan (1751–1812), the ill-fated Revolutionary War hero who met an untimely death after opposing Madison's declaration of war on England. Lingan was one of the original nineteen proprietors who agreed to sell land needed to establish the Federal capital. A prominent Georgetowner, he was collector of the port, and under Adams, a U.S. marshal. He later moved on to Washington and sold the house in 1798 to John Templeman, a one-time president of the Bank of Columbia.

Prospect House has been continuously occupied by locally and nationally prominent families who relished its picturesque location. From 1861 to 1868 it was owned by General William Whiton who shared the house with General D. C. McCallum, who like Whiton was a railroad and bridge engineer in the Union army.

More recently the house was owned by James E. Forrestal, Secretary of the Navy and later first Secretary of Defense in Truman's cabinet. Following Forrestal's suicide in 1949, his widow leased the house to the United States government as a guest house for foreign heads of state while Blair House (see page 19) was occupied by President Truman. Between 1949 and 1951 the house accommodated a succession of prominent personages, including the Shah of Iran and President Vincent Auriol of France.

The architect is said to have been Lingan himself. But, more than likely, Prospect House was designed by a master carpenter whose taste and sense of what would be appropriate would have been derived from James Gibb's *Book of Architecture* (London, 1728), or even adapted from existing house designs. Combined with extremely fine workmanship, the result is one of the most handsome houses in Georgetown.

Retrace your steps to 34th Street.

The same praise cannot be given to **Halcyon House*** at 3400 Prospect Street, which you will pass on your way to M Street. Yet behind this odd facade is one of the grandest mansions in Georgetown, built in 1787 by Benjamin Stoddert, first Secretary of the Navy, wealthy landowner, and merchant extraordinary. Blame it all on the eccen-

Prospect House

tric Albert Adsit Clemens, who bought the property in 1900 and built a shell around the Stoddert house. All he needed was more space for his vast collection of Americana!

Turn left and walk down 34th Street. Before you turn left onto M, glance across at the vacant lot on the south side. The house of Francis Scott Key (author of the national anthem) stood here for many years until it was demolished in 1947 when the Whitehurst Freeway was built. Had the Old Georgetown Act existed then, the historic Key house would have been saved. Now turn left onto the busy M Street strip. The difference in mood and ambience is overwhelming, but continue west on the left-hand side of the street.

Glance across at 3350, the **Forrest-Marbury House*** (now a discotheque), once the house of Uriah Forrest, Revolutionary War general and member of the Continental Congress. It was here on March 29, 1791, that Forrest gave the famous dinner that led to the final agreement between George Washington, his district commissioners, and the landowners to acquire the land needed to establish the new capital city. "The business," wrote Washington in his diary, "being thus happily finished."

It has been said that change has never been a stranger to Georgetown. But in the past it was a leisurely process. One can only regret that so much of historic M Street is owned by individuals willing to rent them to the highest bidder. Perhaps this will not always be so. Historic preservation can often be achieved by adaptive re-use—not merely keeping something as it was, but recycling to alternative uses while keeping the architectural structure intact. One such example was the historic **Market House*** at 3276 M Street, which goes back as far as the Revolutionary period, when a market house replaced the town jail in 1795. The present market was built in 1865 and after many ups and downs was abandoned and finally for twenty years rented to the Southern Auto Supply Company. The old Market House is slated to be restored but what its new function will be has yet to be decided.

A few steps farther on M Street (at 3206) brings you to an example of adaptive re-use in action, **City Tavern***. Originally built in 1796, City Tavern, at the sign of the Indian king, was one of the most popular hostelries in the area, catering to merchants, dignitaries, and government officials. The tavern was a main stage stop on the post road between Philadelphia, then the nation's capital, and Baltimore, Annapolis, Georgetown, Alexandria, Charlottesville, and points south. It was a favorite rendezvous for early nineteenth century VIPs, and banquets were given here for Adams, Jefferson, Jackson, and many other notables.

The tavern's decline began when railroads brought in the modern hotel era; it successively became an oyster house, drugstore, and printshop before ending up in the 1950s as a nondescript store. The old inn had long been forgotten and had been presumed destroyed until a National Park Service historian discovered that it was still standing barely, though recognizable, because of the continual change of ownership and facelifts. What followed was indeed a saga of preservation. By early 1960, the $500,000 needed to restore the building was well on the way to being raised. Two years later the building had been fully restored from prints, plans, and other bits of information discovered through painstaking research. The City Tavern (now a private social club not open to the public) boasts of a tap room, conference room, a library with books by members (including Dean Acheson, Art Buchwald, Walter Lippman, Drew Pearson, Marquis Childs, and Herman Wouk), plus a great dining hall. It is as popular today with Georgetown society as was the old City Tavern a 150 years ago.

You have now completed the tour of Georgetown. At the end of the block, you can cross Wisconsin Avenue and either catch a bus at the stop by the Door Store or collect your car from any of the parking lots.

WALK SIX

Alexandria

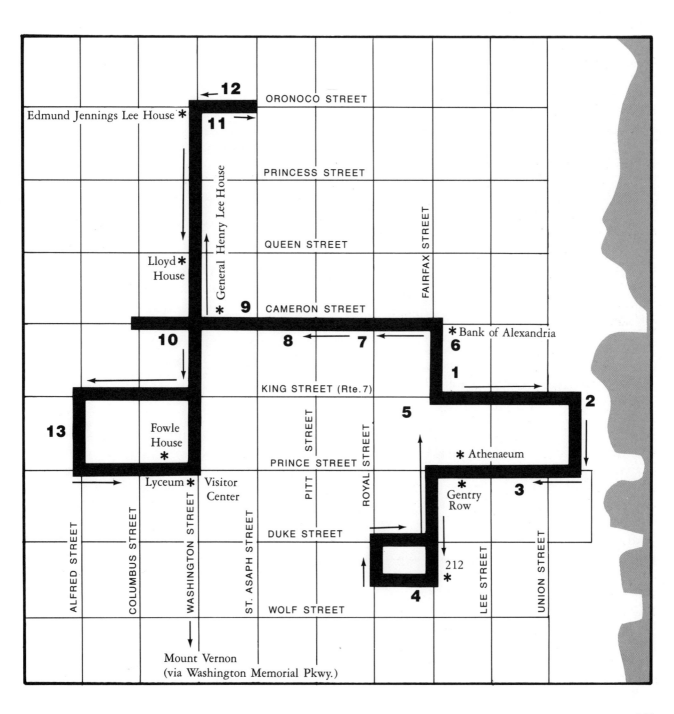

Distance: 4 miles. Time 5–6 hours. If possible, devote one whole day. It can also be done in 2–3 hours, depending on how many buildings are visited. Metrobus: call (202)637-2437 for current bus schedules. Parking: apply at Ramsay House for a free tourist permit that allows parking on metered streets; there are commercial lots on City Hall Square and along Union Street near the waterfront. Restaurants: along King Street between Washington and Union Streets are several good light-food establishments. For more sumptuous dining, ask for the restaurant guide at the Visitors' Center.

Alexandria, formally established in 1749, is one of those historic seaport cities of the Atlantic that has somehow survived decay and, worse, demolition. Five miles down the Potomac from Washington, Alexandria's street names evoke the town's loyalist sentiments in colonial days: King, Queen, Royal, Prince, Princess, and Duke. Its first settlers were hard-headed Scots traders, among them William Ramsay and John Carlyle, who exerted a strong and positive influence upon the new town's development as a thriving, bustling port.

After the Revolution, Alexandria continued to grow. Ships clustered along the wharves loading and unloading cargo to and from ports around the world. Wealthy merchants, planters, and sea captains built fine rowhouses, founded a library, established schools. Alexandria became so prosperous that it was considered a possible site for the new Federal City.

Thanks to timely designation as a Historic District in 1969, almost one hundred blocks comprising more than one thousand restored buildings of this unique old city survive. Walking its tree-shaded, red-brick sidewalks to gaze at (and sometimes enter) its many late eighteenth- and early nineteenth-century edifices is one of the highlights of a visit to Washington. Some of the more notable structures include Carlyle House (1752), a fine Georgian mansion that General Edward Braddock used as his headquarters while preparing for his fateful march into western Maryland and Pennsylvania in 1755 during the French and Indian Wars; Christ Church (1773), a well-preserved colonial church where the Washingtons and the Lees worshiped; Gadsby's Tavern (1792), setting for society balls, meetings of patriots, and receptions for at least six Presidents; Robert E. Lee's boyhood home (1795), a large mid-Georgian colonial mansion where the Confederate general spent much of his boyhood; the Yeaton-Fairfax House (1799–1867), one of the finest Federal mansions of the South; and Captain's Row, a picturesque street of smaller, more intimate houses built by sea captains and tradesmen.

Begin your tour at Ramsay House, Alexandria's official Visitors' Center, operated by the Alexandria Tourist Council, a nonprofit organization funded by the city to promote Alexandria's historic landmarks, travel facilities, and special events. Here, as at the Lyceum, the Bicentennial Visitors' Center, you can obtain information, booklets, maps, reservations, and advice on almost everything about Alexandria and its district.

Ramsay House

221 King Street, Alexandria, Virginia 22314. A National Historic Landmark owned by the Alexandria Tourist Council. Telephone: (703)549-0205. Open daily 10:00 A.M.–4:30 P.M. Closed Thanksgiving, Christmas, and New Year's Day. Time: 20 minutes to see house. Also see free 13-minute color documentary film *Alexandria in Virginia, Washington's Home Town.*

Built in 1724, the **Ramsay House (1)** is Alexandria's oldest. It once served as office and home for William Ramsay, a shrewd and likeable young Scotsman who rose to become one of the town's most illustrious founding fathers and a Revolutionary patriot. Where the house originally stood is unknown, but the gambrel roof type of colonial dwelling can still be found in the Virginia Tidewater region. The original house contained only one room on each floor, but was enlarged to two rooms on each floor before it was moved to its present site in 1749. How the house got here also makes an interesting story.

Young Ramsay, a member of a prominent Edinburgh family with connections in Virginia, arrived in the colonies in the 1740s. Intent on acquiring

Ramsay House

property and making a fortune, he settled first in Dumfries, some thirty miles downriver, where he represented a consortium of Glasgow merchants. Soon he was involved in trading ventures with fellow Scotsmen, especially John Carlyle. Both were among the first trustees of Alexandria and bought lots at the first auction, July 13, 1749.

The ambitious Ramsay lost no time in establishing himself. He floated a small building upriver on a barge and placed it on his lot facing the Potomac.

Long before his fellow trustees had even thought of ordering supplies to build their houses, he had a roof over his head and an office in which to conduct his business affairs. He and his wife, Anne, lived here until their growing family finally forced them to move to a much larger house. But for many years the little house remained in the family before changing ownership and becoming successively tavern, grocery store, rooming house, and, surprisingly, a cigar factory.

Old Fitzgerald Warehouse

William and Anne Ramsay were ardent patriots. He served as town overseer, census taker, postmaster, and member of the Committee of Safety. In 1761 he was made lord mayor and acclaimed as "first projector and founder of this promising city." He was a close personal friend of Washington. The Ramsays entertained the newly-appointed commander of the Continental Army to breakfast when the great man passed through Alexandria to formally accept command.

Anne Ramsay was just as indefatigable as her husband in her support of the struggle for independence; she raised more than $75,000, a huge amount at the time, to promote the war effort. When Ramsay died in 1795, Washington walked behind the coffin to the plaintive nostalgic strain of a Scots lament played by the pipers of the St. Andrew's Society.

Continue down King Street, a prime location for warehouses, inns, and taverns since the town was founded. In New Market Square, on the site now occupied by the Holiday Inn, stood the Marshall House, demolished in 1872, where first blood was drawn at the outbreak of the Civil War. On the morning of May 24, 1861, Colonel Elmer Ellsworth and his New York Zouaves landed to occupy the rebel city. Confederate units had withdrawn the previous week but the Zouaves were determined to rip down a large Confederate flag flying from the Marshall House flagpole. Some hours later, angry soldiers carried the gallant but foolhardy Colonel back to Washington. Shot by James Jackson, the enraged proprietor, who was himself shot dead, Ellsworth was the first man to die for the Union cause.

Old Fitzgerald Warehouse

King and Union Streets. A National Historic Landmark owned by the Seaport Inn and Dockside Sales, Inc.

As you walk down King Street note the old warehouses now occupied by restaurants and shops. The original tenants were shipping merchants, chandlers, sailmakers (who used the high roofed top floors to stretch and repair sails), and riggers, who stored ropes and tackle in the cavernous basements. Pause at the corner of King and Union Streets for a first full view of the Potomac. Opposite, at the northeast corner stands the **Old Fitzgerald Warehouse** (2), once a sail loft, salesroom, and countinghouse for Lyle and Fitzgerald, later Fitzgerald and Peers. It was built about 1760 by John Patterson, an "undertaker" (eighteenth-century Virginian term for building countractor). He certainly built things to last. The walls are a fortress-thick twenty-eight inches, spanned by great adze-hewn beams still in good shape.

John Fitzgerald himself was a genial Irishman, a highly successful shipping merchant who mixed business with pleasure. He was a close friend of Washington (who once described him as "a rock") and served as his aide-de-camp for two years during the Revolutionary War. Afterward a colonel, he lived on nearby Lee Street, dispensing fine brandy to the wits of the town. He owned and rode fine horses and frequently joined Washington to chase the fox. He was mayor of Alexandria, 1787, and collector of customs, 1798 until his death in 1799.

Two hundred years ago, when square-rigged ships from the West Indies and Europe crowded the river, unloading their cargoes of rum and Madeira, sugar and spices, furniture and brocade, the young ladies of Alexandria came here to inspect the latest dress materials and to place orders.

Continue along Union to Prince Street.

Captain's Row

The 100 block of Prince Street between Union and Lee Streets. Private residences not open to the public except on special house tours.

Cross to the left-hand side of Prince and walk up one of the town's oldest streets (laid out in 1749) to view one of the most delightful sights of Alexandria, the picturesque Federal houses known as **Captain's Row** (3). Several of these were built by Captain John Harper (1728–1804), a Philadelphia Quaker shipping merchant who settled here in 1773 to become a prosperous merchant and illustrious citizen. During the years Alexandria rivaled New York and Boston as a port of entry, these houses were owned or occupied by sea captains or masters of ships. After dark when the old street lights cast their shadows on the mellowed brick facades, one can well imagine some bewhiskered sea dog making his way up the steeply angled sidewalk from a nearby wharf, or, more likely, a tavern.

The first house on the northwest corner of Prince and Union overlooking the river was originally the warehouse of Harper and his partner Hartshorne. Harper's Wharf, long since gone, jutted out into the water on the other side of Union Street. The Captain's Quaker principles prevented him from taking up arms to fight for the patriot cause, but when Washington was equipping the militia companies of Prince William and Fairfax Counties, it was Harper who supplied him with powder, drums, and regimental colors.

The industrious Harper was mainly interested in exporting flour to Europe. This must have made him a great deal of money for he bought Walnut Hill, an estate in Fairfax County, and it enabled him to continue building houses well into his old age. Twice married, he had twenty children, and to each and every one he left a house and a lot!

Many of the houses on Captain's Row, or Sea Captain's Row, as it is sometimes called, were spacious enough to be used in part for business. One can well imagine 115, 117, and 119, for example, three immensely tall dormer-windowed houses in the Philadelphia style performing such a dual function. The first floor would be used to show merchandise and the attics for storage, with family quarters on the second floor. This explains the more elaborate woodwork and plaster ceilings found in second-floor

Captain's Row

rooms. My favorites are 123 and 127, almost at the end of the block. Number 123 is a handsome residence built by Harper in 1795 for his sons-in-law, John Crips Vowell and Thomas Vowell, Jr., also involved in the shipping business. Known as the Harper-Vowell House, it boasts, according to the Alexandria historian Gay Montague Moore, one of the most unusual interiors in the town, a remarkable French Directory style tent-ceilinged room. A finely wrought iron fence adds the finishing touch to this superb little house. The house at 127 was built a year later, in 1796, by Aloysius and Joseph Boone. It was later owned by the Fitzhugh family until 1867. Notice the shutters, or blinds, at the entrance doors of both houses, a distinctly characteristic feature of Alexandria houses of the Federal era.

Slightly farther up the street on the corner of Prince and Lee Streets is the eye-catching antebellum **Athenaeum***, 201 Prince Street. Telephone: (703)548-0035. Open Tuesday through Saturday 10:00 A.M.–4:00 P.M. Sunday 1:00–4:00 P.M.. Free. Regular exhibit program and museum shop. Time: 15 minutes.

Originally this handsome Greek Revival building (architect unknown) housed the Bank of the Old Dominion. It was built 1851–1852 as a banking house, conveniently located near the busy waterfront and the countinghouse of shipping merchants. The vivid combination of pumpkin and cream were the original colors before the Civil War, according to the National Park Service, which made a study of the exterior surface at the request of the Northern Virginia Arts Association. However, a Brady photograph of 1864 shows the building decorated in the fashionable ashlar, or square-hewn stone effect, with fine white lines to represent mortar between the painted stone blocks.

The Bank of the Old Dominion was Confederate in its loyalties, and thereby hangs a tale. Lincoln's election as President of the United States touched off the secession of the South. When Federal troops occupied Alexandria on May 24, 1861, Old Dominion, anticipating confiscation of its assets, promptly closed its doors for the duration. Later that night, cashier William Henry Lambert gathered up precious documents and papers from the vaults, loaded them in a wagon, and drove off to a place known only to himself and Robert Miller, president of the bank. Lambert buried the records, but dug them up after the war ended and paid off his obligations to former customers.

Alexandria's prosperity ended with the Civil War. Fewer and fewer ships anchored in the Potomac, until little remained to show that the town once was a bustling port. The next owners were the Free Methodist Church, and then in 1963 it too vacated the building, which subsequently was offered for sale to the highest bidder. Fortunately, preservation-minded citizens joined forces to buy the building and renovate it as an anthenaeum, that uniquely Victorian institution, and association of persons of literary, scientific, an artistic attainment and patrons of learning.

Just beyond the Athenaeum is the 200 block of Prince Street, known as **Gentry Row*** in deference one might think to the various leading citizens of the past who lived here. But no, the label is a relatively new one. As on Captain's Row, these are private residences; they have, however, been opened frequently to the public on special house tours. The more outstanding include:

207: Built by William Fairfax, one of the original trustees of Alexandria. It was inherited by his son, George William Fairfax (1730–1811); a contemporary of Washington, he accompanied him on a 1748 surveying trip into what was then the wilderness country around Winchester, Virginia. Fairfax served for a time as a member of the House of Burgesses in Williamsburg. He had been educated in England, where he had many friends and relatives. As a Tory he refused to be associated with the mounting tide of dissent against the London government. Finally in 1771, sensing what was to come, he sold the house to Robert Adam and returned to England with his wife to remain there permanently.

Adam, a prominent merchant and also a town trustee, came to Alexandria as a young man from Scotland in 1760 and became a partner of John Carlyle. Carlyle and Adam acted as agents for the Mount Vernon estate, handling all the wheat and tobacco grown there by Washington. But he had only a passing interest in the property and sold the house to the sharp-witted Captain John Harper in 1773.

The English radical William Hodgson was the next owner. A staunch supporter of the American cause, Hodgson was a member of the Royal Society and the Honest Whigs, a London supper club of which Benjamin Franklin was a prominent member. After serving a two-year sentence in Newgate jail for toasting the French republic and calling George III "a German hogbutcher," Hodgson arrived in America with a letter of introduction to Washington. Two years later he bought 207 Prince Street and established a flourishing dry-goods business, using the first floor for his merchandise and office and the upper part for himself and his family. The Hodgsons lived here for thirteen years before the house was sold to John Gardner Ladd, another shipping merchant.

209, 211, and 213: Built by Captain Harper, who also built many of the houses seen earlier on Captain's Row. Erected about 1786–1793, together with 207 and 215, they make the most impressive eighteenth-century street in Alexandria. The house at 209 was built about 1786 and was the captain's own house and later inherited by his daughter Elizabeth; 211 was a gift in trust for his daughter Peggy, who also got 213. The houses were later owned or occupied by celebrated local figures, notably Dr. James Craik and Dr. Elisha Cullen Dick. Craik, who lived at 209 for a time, was a famous physician who attended Washington during his final illness. As surgeon-general he accompanied Washington in every battle he fought during the Revolution, ending with Yorktown. But he was unable to save him from the fateful throat infection, now thought to have been inflammatory edema of the larynx. Local historians state that the plaque on 209 properly belongs to 211 because recently discovered deeds reveal that 211 was the home of Dr. Dick until 1820.

Dr. Elisha Cullen Dick, a relative of Sir Alexander Dick, president of the Royal College of Physicians of Edinburgh, and host to Dr. Johnson on his celebrated visit to that city, had completed his medical training there at the close of the Revolutionary War. He was, therefore, a younger colleague of Craik, who called him in for consultation during the last day of Washington's illness. Dick was a highly cultured man and was particularly interested in public health problems. He served as public health officer and identified the major causes of yellow fever, cholera, and smallpox. He drafted local regulations to control these ravaging diseases, the result of polluted drinking water and infected persons entering the town from foreign ports.

Old Presbyterian Meetinghouse

Old Presbyterian Meetinghouse

321 South Fairfax Street. A National Historic Landmark. Telephone: (703)549-6670. Open Monday through Friday 9:00 A.M.–4:00 P.M. Inquire at church office for summer hours. Sunday service: 11:00 A.M. Time: 15 minutes.

Retrace your steps to the intersection of Prince and Lee Streets. Proceed south on Lee to Wolfe Street. Turn right on Wolfe, then right again on South Fairfax Street. At 212 South Fairfax, opposite Old Presbyterian, lived another of George Washington's physicians, Dr. William Brown (1748–1792) who, like his fellow Scot, Dr. Craik, was a graduate of the University of Edinburgh. He served as physician-general and director of hospitals of the Continental Army through the Revolutionary War and was the author of the first American *Pharmacopeia* (1778).

Directly opposite is the venerable facade of **Old Presbyterian Meetinghouse (4)**, which played an important role in the lives of many prominent figures in the early history of the United States.

Alexandria, like much of Virginia, was settled by a massive Scots immigration after the suppression of the revolts of 1715 and 1745 in support of the Stuart Pretenders to the English throne. The majority sought land to farm, and pushed on into the trackless wilderness, moving down the Shenandoah Valley of Virginia to the Carolinas and Georgia. Merchants, sea captains, and professional men—among them early leaders of Alexandria—remained in the Tidewater region and went into business. They brought with them the democratic Presbyterian faith of the Scots middle class.

Known in colonial and Revolutionary days as "Old First," the plain old church was completed in 1774 by John Carlyle, the builder of Christ Church. Its simple, commodious interior reflects the Presbyterian preference for an amphitheater or lecture-hall plan, with the pulpit as the focus.

Old Presbyterian has been called the Masonic Westminster Abbey because of its many historical associations with the Freemasons of the Revolutionary period. Here in 1783 was held the first religious meeting of the lodge of which George Washington was the worshipful master, and in succeeding years, the anniversary of St. John the Evangelist was commemorated in Masonic Fashion, with Washington attending many of the ceremonies. Walk on through the churchyard. Here lie many prominent Alexandrians, all members of the lodge. Among them is Dr. James Craik, who administered to General Braddock as he lay dying after the ambush at Monongahela during his fateful campaign. Here also lie John Carlyle, builder of Carlyle House, one of the most illustrious citizens of colonial America (see page 123); William Hunter, Jr., founder of the St. Andrew Society of Alexandria; and Captain John Harper (see above).

Exit on Royal Street and turn right. Proceed to Duke. Turn right on Duke and left on Fairfax to King Street.

Stabler-Leadbeater Apothecary Shop

105 South Fairfax Street. A museum and consignment antique giftshop maintained and operated by the Landmark Society of Old Alexandria. Telephone: (703)836-3713. Open Monday through Saturday 10:00 A.M.–4:30 P.M. Free audio tour. Time: 15 minutes; more if you are a bottle buff.

Just before the intersection of South Fairfax and King Streets is the old **Stabler-Leadbeater Apothecary Shop (5)**, which opened for business in 1792. When the shop closed in 1938 it was the second oldest in the United States in continuous operation. The historic old curiosity shop was then acquired by the Landmark Society, and its remarkable contents purchased by the American Pharmaceutical Association.

In the eighteenth and early nineteenth centuries, pills, tablets, capsules, and other medicines were made up by the druggist. Quaker Edward Stabler was unusually successful in his performance of the exacting task. Within a year of establishing himself, he had not only repaid the loan of $500 with which he had started the business but had also doubled his stock. After his death in 1831 his son, William, took charge, as did other Stabler sons until John Leadbeater (who married Stabler's daughter in 1835) took over in 1852. John died in 1860 and the business was continued by Leadbeater sons, grandsons, and great-grandsons in unbroken family ownership up until 1933.

How distinguished some of their customers were is indicated by the correspondence, a selection of which can be seen in the old store. At least seven generations of the Washington and Lee families, related by blood or marriage, dealt with Stabler and Leadbeater. These include George and Martha Washington and continued through her grandson, George Washington Parke Custis; the latter's daughter, Mrs. Robert E. Lee; their son, General William Lee; and many other members of that extraordinary cavalier family.

During the War of 1812 the apothecary shop was ransacked. Because Alexandria had no military force it was defenseless against the might of the Royal Navy. A British naval squadron commanded by Captain James Gordon anchored off the port in the

Potomac while Washington burned. The Committee of Vigilance was afraid it would be Alexandria's turn next. On August 29, 1814, the British turned their guns on the town and delivered an ultimatum that all goods intended for export be surrendered and all naval stores be handed over. A local merchant, William Wilson, was chosen to be spokesman. His firm had close commercial ties with England but Captain Gordon remained unimpressed. Finally, Mayor Charles Sims capitulated, and for the next three days sailors loaded flour, beef, and tobacco from Alexandria's bulging warehouses. The Stabler-Leadbeater store did not escape, and large supplies of drugs and medicines were carried off to the British ships.

The drugstore was a meeting place not only of the gentlemen of the town but Washington politicans. Distinguished Congressmen like Clay, Webster, and Calhoun frequently journeyed by ferry to Alexandria to dine with Phineas Janney, a well-known merchant famous for his dinner table and excellent wines. While waiting for the ferry to return to Washington, they gathered in the old drugstore to swap yarns or discuss events of the day, filling their long clay pipes from a huge jar of tobacco on the counter. Sometimes a "drap" was indulged in, as the law of the time did not forbid the dispensing of alcoholic beverages by druggists.

Before he assumed command of the Confederate army, Robert E. Lee (1807–1870) was also a *habitué*. On October 16, 1859, seated in his favorite Windsor chair (still there), he was chatting with John Leadbeater when Lieutenant Jeb Stuart strode in with spurs ringing to hand him an order. It instructed Colonel Lee to command a contingent of marines at Harper's Ferry to put down the rebellion led by abolitionist John Brown. "I'm afraid," exclaimed Lee, in one of history's classic understatements, "this will be followed by some serious trouble."

During the Civil War Stabler, a Quaker, declined to take the oath of allegiance to the Union. The store was closed for a short time while he considered offering his services to Lee for assignment to the medical corps of the Confederate Army. But he decided otherwise and was on duty in the store when he heard the sounds of battle in the distance. Although it was now illegal to sell liquor to soldiers, he passed out the famous substitute known as "hot drops" to Union troops in retreat from the battlefield of Bull Run. Known officially as Leadbeater's Lubri-

Stabler-Leadbeater Apothecary Shop

cation Liniment, it became a staple beverage among the boys in blue.

Continue across King Street to Carlyle House.

Carlyle House

Carlyle House

121 North Fairfax Street. A National Historic Landmark. Telephone: (703)549-2997. Open Tuesday through Saturday 10:00 A.M.–5:00 P.M. Sunday 12:00 NOON–5:00 P.M. Closed Christmas Eve, Christmas and New Year's. Admission: adults, $2.00, $1.50 for senior citizens; ages 6–17, $1.00, under 6, free. Special group rates. Guided tour every half hour, last tour at 4:30 P.M. Time: 40 minutes.

On the east side of North Fairfax, between King and Cameron Streets, stands **Carlyle House (6)**. This handsome stone mansion, with its hip-on-hip roof is an outstanding example of colonial Georgian architecture. It was built between 1751 and 1753 as the home of John Carlyle (1720–1780), who came to Virginia from his native Scotland around 1740 in the hopes of making a fortune independent of the family estate, which, under English law of primogeniture, had been passed to his older brother. A resounding success at his chosen profession, Carlyle eventually became a partner in two Alexandria merchant firms—the firm of Carlyle and Dalton specialized in the West Indies trade, and the firm of Adam & Co. concentrated their enterprises on the lucrative wheat and flour trade. Carlyle became one of Alexandria's leading citizens.

Carlyle's success in business was matched by his good luck in winning the hand of Sarah Fairfax of Belvoir Manor. Sarah's father was not only one of the most influential men in the colony of Virginia but also manager of his cousin's (the powerful Thomas Lord Fairfax) vast estate in England. With this social advantage, Carlyle emerged as a leading figure who counted Washington among his friends. A founding trustee of Alexandria, he was the town's first overseer and later a justice of Fairfax County Court.

Carlyle set out to build a mansion worthy of his new wife and his standing in the community. Carlyle almost certainly designed his house using architectural pattern books or folio plates for inspiration; he may have derived his design from William Adam's plans for Craigiehall, a country house that still stands south of Edinburgh. Carlyle House is unusual in that it is the only country-style house built in eighteenth-century Alexandria. Set high above the Potomac, Carlyle House once dominated Alexandria's busy waterfront.

In April 1755 an historic episode took place at Carlyle House. It was here that General Braddock met with Governors Dinwiddie of Virginia, Sharpe of Maryland, Morris of Pennsylvania, Delancey of New York, and Shirley of Massachusetts to plan the ill-conceived campaign against the French and the Indians along the Ohio River. Because of his experience in coping with the French the previous year in the Great Meadows campaign, the young Washington, then a twenty-three-old militia commander, was invited to join Braddock's staff as a volunteer aide. Braddock, a sixty-year-old veteran but a military traditionalist, was confident of an easy victory. But the French, who had learned much about forest warfare from their Indian allies, shot Braddock and his men down like ninepins. Half the expedition, including Braddock, fell. The survivors, ably commanded by the young Washington, retreated in good order. During the Revolutionary War, Carlyle served on the Fairfax Committee of Safety and lost his only son at the Battle of Eutaw Springs.

After Carlyle died in 1780, the house passed to his daughter, Sarah, and her husband, William Herbert, president of the Bank of Alexandria. Herbert erected the bank's new building in 1807 on the Carlyle property. In 1827 ownership of the house was transferred; the house fell into disrepair until James Green, a local manufacturer, purchased and remodeled it as his family home. He also converted the defunct Bank of Alexandria building into a hotel, making extensive additions that obscured the gracious old mansion from public view. After Green sold out in 1882, Carlyle House served a variety of functions (Baedeker's *United States* of 1893 describes it as the old Carey House). In 1906 the house was purchased by Humphrey Wager; after undergoing a "colonial restoration," the house was opened as a museum. Threatened with demolition, the old mansion was saved at the eleventh hour by Lloyd Schaffer, who acquired the property just before World War II and established a house museum there. Finally, in 1969, Carlyle House was purchased by the Northern Virginia Regional Park Authority and restored. Although some of the stripping verged on overkill, the rescue of the historic old house is a remarkable achievement.

Continue now on North Fairfax. Notice the **Bank of Alexandria*** on the northwest corner of Fairfax and Cameron Streets, completed in 1807 to house the first chartered bank in Virginia. The bank's stockholders and clients included the town's most prominent families. After the bank's failure during the panic of 1834, it was used as a U.S. post office and customs house before being converted to Green's Mansion House Hotel. During the Civil War it was used as a hospital.

Now turn left on Cameron and walk a block to Royal Street. A left turn onto Royal will bring you face to face with the celebrated Gadsby's Tavern.

Gadsby's Tavern

134 North Royal Street. A National Historic Landmark owned and operated by the City of Alexandria. Telephone: (703)838-4242. Open Tuesday through Saturday 10:00 A.M.– 5:00 P.M., Sunday 1:00–5:00 P.M. Closed major holidays. Admission: adults, $2.00; ages 6–17, $1.00. Guided tour. Last tour each day 4:15 P.M. Time: 30 minutes.

On the southwest corner of North Royal and Cameron Streets, stands the imposing **Gadsby's Tavern** (7), one of the most historic inns in the United States. It is really two distinctly separate buildings. The smaller of the two, late Georgian in style, was built in 1770 and was known successively as City Tavern, the Bunch of Grapes and Fountain Tavern. The adjoining Federal building, famous for its great ballroom, was built by businessman John Wise in 1792 as the City Hotel.

Situated on the main stage route, near the King's Highway, from Boston to Williamsburg, the tavern was a convenient meeting place. During the period prior to the Revolutionary War (1775–1783), it became an important political and social center.

In 1796 the City Hotel was taken over by John Gadsby, a shrewd and handsome Englishman whose first venture in town had been a waterfront tavern and coffeehouse for merchants and sea captains. He signed a six-year lease with Wise for the large building. When he renewed it in 1802, the lease included the adjoining City Tavern building.

Gadsby saw the need for superior accommodations close to the raw and rapidly changing Federal City. As excellent as the service had been under Wise, it now reached even greater heights of comfort and *bonne cuisine*. So much so that the middle- and upper-class traveler usually made sure to stay at Gadsby's before braving the mosquito-plagued capital.

Gadsby's enjoyed a long boom and fed the famous for more than a century. The great ballroom became the venue of brilliant Presidential banquets and balls

Gadsby's Tavern

124

honoring Washington's birth and celebrating the Fourth of July and other patriotic occasions. Washington's birthday celebration is still a yearly affair. Washington himself dined here many times throughout his busy life. It was here at Gadsby's in 1798 that he made his last military appearance. After a sumptuous feast of canvas-back duck and hominy, washed down with Madeira, Port, and brandy, the aging soldier-President stood on the front steps of the larger building to review the Alexandria Independent Infantry Blues, a company of volunteers; it was his last military review of the troops.

The register of other distinguished guests who enjoyed the hospitality of Gadsby's reads like a "Who's Who" of illustrious Americans. They include John Adams, John Quincy Adams, Clinton, Jefferson, the Lees, the Masons, and the Washingtons, besides such distinguished visitors as the Marquis de Lafayette.

For many years a legend has been attached to Gadsby's, which concerns a veiled, unnamed rich invalid who is said to have died in the tavern rooms in the nineteenth century. The story is entirely conjectural, but its survival today suggests the continuity between modern Alexandrians and the post-Revolutionary townsmen whose imaginations have been piqued by a mysterious lady.

John Gadsby left Alexandria for greener pastures and established successful hotels in Baltimore and Washington. He became so wealthy that in 1836 he bought the celebrated Decatur House on Lafayette Square. Here, after a life devoted to serving the social and political establishment, he died at seventy-four.

The glory of Gadsby's gradually disappeared as the historic old tavern passed through a succession of owners just before and after the Civil War. Finally in 1878 it closed. By 1917 the building was threatened with demolition; its front door, mantels, and ballroom woodwork were bought by the Metropolitan Museum of Art. In 1929 the tavern was purchased by the American Legion Post 24. The Legion saved the buildings from demolition and with other local organizations did much to bring about its first restoration. The ballroom woodwork of the 1792 building still belongs to the Metropolitan, but it has been replaced by an exact copy. The main front doorcase was repurchased from the Metropolitan in 1949, and the facade restored.

In 1972 the Legion donated the buildings to the City of Alexandria. After thorough research, the entire complex was restored to its 1770–1810 appearance. A small portion of the large building now functions as a working restaurant and tavern; the rest is Gadsby's Tavern Museum, which should not be missed.

Today the tavern flourishes as it did in Gadsby's day. Its taprooms and dining rooms have been restored to their original state. Museum events recreate the activities of eighteenth-century tavern life. Lunch and dinner are served by young people in colonial attire.

Before leaving the tavern to walk down Cameron Street to our next site, Washington's Townhouse, notice the tavern ice well, down steps on the Cameron Street side. Underground ice wells were used in the eighteenth and nineteenth centuries to store ice for summer use. Gadsby's ice well is a large and rare urban example.

George Washington's Townhouse

508 Cameron Street. Private residence.

Cross to the north side of Cameron Street to view **George Washington's Townhouse (8)**, a 1960 replica of a modest eighteenth-century dwelling that stood on the site, 1765–1854. Washington purchased the lot and built the house with stabling to provide convenient quarters for those occasions when business or inclement weather prevented his return to Mount Vernon and as a guesthouse for his family or friends. The young Dr. William Brown lived here for some time and it was also made available to Washington's nephew, Bushrod Washington.

Because country houses of prominent Revolutionary leaders were often raided by the crews of British men-of-war during the Revolutionary War, Washington considered moving his family to the Alexandria townhouse from Mount Vernon. The danger soon passed, however, and the house remained as it was, a family *pied-a-terre*. After Washington's death in 1799, Martha left it to a nephew who promptly sold it.

In 1855 it was destroyed by fire. Fortunately, a history-minded neighbor, Miss Mary Stewart, who

George Washington's Townhouse

Fairfax House

Peter Hogarth
Yeaton-Fairfax House, Alexandria

at one time had lived across the street, made a detailed, if crudely drawn, sketch that later became the basis of a restoration by the Washington architect Deering Davis for the former governor of Guam, Richard Barrett Lowe, and his wife.

Although a replica, the little house has mellowed to the degree where it is possible to accept it as a tribute to the memory of the great man.

Recross Cameron and continue west toward Christ Church to the **Fairfax House (9)** at 607 Cameron Street. Private residence.

The Fairfax House or, as it is sometimes called, the Yeaton-Fairfax House, is a large, stylish residence built around 1803 by William Yeaton, a New Hampshire merchant and shipowner who came to Alexandria about 1800 and established himself as master builder and architect. The house is an unusual variation of the Georgian or Federal style.

As a rule, houses were an excellent investment in colonial and Federal America. And plenty of people had money to invest along the Atlantic seaboard; savings were accumulating as a result of the expansion of domestic and foreign trade. Yeaton, a man of considerable skill (he also designed and built the Washington home, Mount Vernon), decided that designing and building houses were more to his liking than commerce, and although he lacked formal training, adapted the Palladian Georgian idiom to local conditions. Books helped such men enormously; builders and carpenters subscribed to the spate of publications compiled by craftsmen for craftsmen published in London from 1715 onward.

In 1830 the house became the winter home of Thomas, the ninth Lord Fairfax, and remained in the Fairfax family for thirty-four years. Thomas was the direct descendant of Thomas, the third Lord Fairfax (1612–1671), the celebrated English soldier-statesman who in the English civil war was given command of the new model army, which he led to victory against Charles I at Naseby.

Thomas was also the descendant of Thomas, the sixth Lord Fairfax (1693–1781), proprietor of 5 million acres of land between the Rappahannock and the Potomac that he inherited through his mother from his grandfather, the second Baron Culpeper, a colonial governor of Virginia. The sixth Lord Fairfax is best remembered for the kindness he showed to a tall, sixteen-year-old boy who had lost his father at such an early age. The boy, of course, was George Washington. Both shared an interest in surveying. While riding together on hunting expeditions or exploring the then wild frontier territory, Fairfax imparted much that would influence Washington in later life. Loyalist in sentiment (he was the only resident peer in the colonies), the tall, gaunt aristocrat went unmolested during the Revolution and ended his days in seclusion at Greenway Court near Winchester, Virginia. But he continued to use the house on Cameron Street as a winter residence until his death in 1846.

Dr. Orlando Fairfax inherited the house from his father, Thomas, the ninth Lord Fairfax, and lived here with his family from 1848–1864. During those years the handsome old mansion was one of the most important salons of Alexandria. The Fairfaxes were the leading family of Virginia. They intermarried with the Carlyles, Washingtons, Herberts, and Carys. Gay Montague Moore, to whom I am indebted for this background account of the family, relates that their contribution to Alexandria was a great one. In their personal lives and public service, they set an example of chivalry and courage. They had great wealth and used it generously, only to lose it for what they believed in. As Dr. Orlando Fairfax was an active supporter of the Confederacy, his house and property were confiscated under an act of Congress. Fortunately for Dr. Orlando, arrangements were made by Governor Morris of New York, his brother-in-law, for the return of the property after the war ended. Meanwhile, members of the family left for Richmond, where they endured a great deal of personal misfortune. The family is represented in England today by Thomas, the thirteenth Lord Fairfax, the great-great-great grandson of Thomas, the ninth Lord Fairfax.

At 611 Cameron Street stands the **General Henry Lee House*** where Henry Lee (1756–1818), father of Confederate General Robert E. Lee, lived from 1799 to 1812 with his second wife, Ann Hill Carter of Shirley, and their five children. A great Revolutionary cavalry leader, Henry, or "Light-Horse Harry," joined the Continental Army at nineteen. He fought in the Northern Campaign, 1775–1777, and, under General Nathanael Greene, the Southern Campaign, 1778–1781, where he led a famous cavalry unit, Lee's Legions. From 1791 to 1794 he was governor of Virginia. Imprisoned for debt, he had a brief rekindling of the old days of glory when he valiantly helped defend the offices of the Baltimore *Federal Republican* against an anti-Federalist mob during the War of 1812.

Christ Church

Southeast corner of Cameron and Columbus Streets. A National Historic Landmark owned by Fairfax Episcopal Parish. Office and Parish House at 118 North Washington Street. Open daily 9:00 A.M.–5:00 P.M., Sundays 2:00–5:00 P.M. Free guided tour. Time: 15–20 minutes.

Walking across North Washington Street to **Christ Church (10)**, we come upon one of the most picturesque sights of old Alexandria. An excellent example of the small rectangular Georgian church, the most popular type in the colonial south, it was designed by James Wren who, as far as I know, was not related to Christopher. Wren, a member of the Fairfax Parish vestry, drew a single set of plans for the two churches—one in Falls Church; the other, Alexandria—that the Fairfax Parish had decided to build. The church was partly built by James Parson; Carlyle who, besides being in the shipping business was also a building contractor, completed it in 1773.

Although not a professional architect, Wren designed a well-proportioned structure. He used his pattern books with discrimination to produce a design of great serenity. The broad-hipped shingled roof, the high, two-tier Palladian window framed by pilasters and a broken pediment of the Tuscan order, the arch-headed windows, all typical features of Georgian architecture, are balanced by large masses of dark Virginia brick laid in English and Flemish bond. The three-story tower with belfry topped by a cupola was completed in 1818. Flanked by great shade trees, the old graveyard where so many prominent citizens are buried includes several Puritan markers probably carved in New England and brought here from Boston.

Intimate, yet dignified, the interior, with its freshly painted white woodwork, contains fine Doric columns and symmetrically aligned pews and benches. A canopied, raised pulpit is centered before the Palladian window.

The church has many associations with George Washington who played a part in the building of the church. He was an original pewholder. Number 60 is the one where he and Martha worshiped. Washington was greatly attached to Christ Church and made a point of attending services here at momentous points in his busy life. He attended Sunday

Christ Church

Lee-Fendall House

service just before leaving for Philadelphia to take command of the Continental Army in May 1775, and on Christmas Day 1783 he attended the service immediately after he had resigned as general of the army. From 1785 onward, he regularly attended services.

As a boy, Robert E. Lee also attended Christ Church, and continued to do so whenever he was in residence at Arlington House. A silver marker on the altar rail shows that he knelt there when he was confirmed in 1853.

Return to north Washington Street.

Lee-Fendall House

614 Oronoco Street. Listed on the National Register of Historic Places. Owned by the Virginia Trust for Historic Preservation. Telephone: (703)548-1789. Open Tueday through Sunday 10:00 A.M.–4:00 P.M. Closed Mondays and holidays. Admission: adults $2.00, students 6–16 $1.00. Guided tour: 20 minutes.

Turn right on Washington Street and walk north to Oronoco Street. At the corner of Washington and Queen Streets we pass 220 North Washington

Street, the dignified facade of the restored **Lloyd House***, built in 1793 by James Hooe and a fine example of mid-Georgian colonial architecture. The house was used by Benjamin Hallowell, an influential Quaker schoolmaster, to house his second school, but on the death of Mrs. Hooe, it was sold in 1832 to John Lloyd, whose wife, Anne Harriot Lee, was a first cousin of Robert E. Lee who, with his wife and children, was a frequent guest of their relatives.

Robert E. Lee was informed of his appointment as commander of the army of Virginia by the state legislature when he stopped here on his way home to Arlington from Christ Church. The house now houses the Rare Book Library of the city of Alexandria.

At the southeast corner of North Washington and Oronoco Streets is the **Lee-Fendall House (11)**, the first of three eighteenth-century houses where members of the famous Virginia Lee family lived. The house was built by Phillip Richard Fendall (grandson of Squire Lee of Blenheim, Maryland) in 1785 on a lot purchased from Henry "Light-Horse Harry" Lee the previous year. Fendall was a director of the Potomac Canal Company and one of the founders of the Bank of Alexandria. More remarkably, he had three wives, *all* Lees! His third was Mary, "Light-Horse Harry's" sister.

George Washington and "Light-Horse Harry" were regular visitors. It was here that Harry wrote a farewell speech from the citizens of Alexandria to Washington. Later, he penned the famous words, "First in war, first in peace, and first in the hearts of his countrymen," for Washington's funeral oration.

The house was lived in from 1785 to 1903 by several generations of the ubiquitous Lees and contains a large collection of furniture, works of art, and memorabilia of various members of that celebrated and controversial family. I was particularly interested in the portrait of the testy Arthur Lee, the Edinburgh-educated lawyer whose envy of Franklin threatened the reputation of the great man and jeopardized the negotiations for the treaty of alliance with France during the Revolution.

More recently the historic old house was the home of the labor leader John L. Lewis from 1937 to 1969.

Lee's Boyhood Home

Across the street at 607 Oronoco Street, is the Fitzhugh-Lee House, or **The Boyhood Home of Robert E. Lee (12)**. A National Historic Landmark owned by the Lee-Jackson Foundation. Open daily 10:00 A.M.–4:00 P.M. Admission: adults $2.00, ages 6–17, $1.00. Guided tour. Time: 30 minutes.

The house has been associated with historic events and personalities from Revolutionary days, even before Henry "Light-Horse Harry" Lee came to live here in 1812. It is one of a pair begun by John Potts in 1793, and completed in 1795, then sold in 1799 to Colonel William Fitzhugh. Both houses, Federal in style, are characterized by their widely spaced windows and long, gabled roofs, each separated by small pediments embellished by oval windows. Fitzhugh served as a member of the Virginia House of Burgesses, the Revolutionary conventions of 1775 and 1776, and of the Continental Congress. Washington was frequently a guest here.

Henry Lee moved his family here from the Lee ancestral home of Stratford in 1812. Because of ill health he left in 1813 for Barbados, believing that a warm climate might restore him. Mrs. Lee remained in the house on Oronoco Street to raise her six children. Henry Lee died on the way home in 1818 and was buried on Cumberland Island off the coast of Georgia at the home of the daughter of his commander, Nathanael Greene.

It was in the Boyhood Home, in the elegant drawing room, that Mrs. Lee, then a widow, received Lafayette during his visit to Alexandria in October 1824. Benjamin Hallowell, a Quaker schoolmaster who had recently moved into the house next door with his bride, stood in the doorway as Lafayette passed on his way to call on Mrs. Lee.

Anne Hill Carter Lee's fourth son was Robert Edward Lee, named for his mother's two favorite brothers, Robert and Edward Carter. Nurtured by the memory of a strong and gallant father and the wise and gentle teachings of a loving mother, Robert E. Lee was to become the greatest and most beloved of leaders, respected by North and South alike for his integrity.

At the time of his father's death, Robert was eleven. After receiving his primary education at the Alexandria Academy, he studied mathematics for West Point at Benjamin Hallowell's School next door. He left for West Point in June 1825, and Mrs.

Lee's Boyhood Home

Lee left soon after to live with her older son, Carter, then a young lawyer in Georgetown. Robert E. Lee never forgot his boyhood home. After the Civil War ended he returned to Alexandria to visit family and friends. The story is told that the new owners of the house on Oronoco Street were startled to see the general walking about the garden. "I wanted to see," he apologized, "if the snowballs were in bloom." Today the garden retains a richly nostalgic ambience, as does the house, possibly because of the great care that has been taken to furnish it in the style of the years it was occupied by Anne Hill Carter Lee and her children.

After Mrs. Lee left, the house passed through the hands of a succession of owners. William Hodgson and his family owned it for two generations before selling to William Yeaton. Recent owners have included the former Empress Zita and her son, the Archduke Otto of the former Austro-Hungarian Empire, and during World War II, the poet Archibald MacLeish.

Cross Washington Street to the **Edmund Jennings Lee House*** at 428 North Washington Street. Private residence; not open to the public. Edmund, unlike his older brother Harry, was a shrewd, level-headed lawyer and churchman. He was very much involved with the affairs of Christ Church, which he successfully represented after the Revolutionary War when the state of Virginia moved to confiscate the glebe lands, set aside in colonial days for the use of various parish churches, usually Anglican. Later, he was mayor of Alexandria, 1815–1821.

Now retrace your steps and walk south to King Street. Turn right on King to Alfred Street, then left to our next stop, the Friendship Firehouse.

Friendship Fire Engine Company

Friendship Fire Engine Company

107 South Alfred Street. Open Tuesday through Saturday 10:00 A.M.–5:00 P.M. Free. Guided tour. Time: 15 minutes.

On the west side of South Alfred Street is the endearingly gawky fire house of the **Friendship Fire Company (13)**, built in 1855.

During the eighteenth century nothing was feared more than fire. As early as 1752 the town trustees ordered that all wooden buildings be replaced with brick or stone structures. To prevent and control such disastrous outbreaks, citizens formed themselves into companies of firefighters. The oldest of those, organized in 1774, was the Friendship Volunteers. It is still in existence and must be the most distinguished volunteer department in the United States. Members have included Presidents, governors, and other celebrities. But unlike the original members, they don't have to put out fires. The top floor is used for their twice yearly celebrations.

Washington himself was a member. On display in the museum is the Philadephia-style hand-pump fire engine he purchased with his own money as a gift to the Friendship Volunteers while he was at the First Continental Congress in Philadelphia in 1774. Also on display here is a second fire engine, purchased in 1849, axes belonging to Washington, and leather handmade buckets, fire helmets, and capes of the original members.

From the firehouse, continue south to Prince Street. Turn east and walk a block. At 711 Prince Street is the handsome **William Fowle House***, private residence. Fowle, a Bostonian, came to Alexandria in 1800 as a partner in the shipping company that subsequently became Lawrason and Fowle, and, finally, William Fowle & Company. He was a president of the Alexandria Canal Company as well as of the Old Dominion Bank. He married Esther Taylor and fathered a massive brood (eighteen children). Fowle was a typical merchant of the Federal era, and the family lived in great style, as this elegantly appointed house indicates. Ethelyn Cox states that family tradition credits the facade to Bulfinch, and certainly the superb entrance is a work of art in itself. Four slender, fluted Doric columns support a cast-iron balcony wrought with almost filigree finesse. The doorcase has engaged columns and a semicircular fanlight above a six-paneled door that is further embellished by an exquisite pair of side windows.

Continue along Prince to South Washington Street. Turn south. At the corner is the **Lyceum***, 201 South Washington Street. Open daily 9:00 A.M.–5:00 P.M. Free.

Long the center of the town's cultural scene, the Greek Revival Lyceum was built jointly by the Alexandria Lyceum Company, founded in 1834 by Hallowell, and the Alexandria Library Company. During the Civil War it was requisitioned as a hospital for Union wounded and did not perform its original function again until 1969 when it was saved from demolition by the city of Alexandria. Part of the building houses exhibits from which much can be learned about colonial Northern Virginia and old Alexandria.

From here you can walk north to Washington and King Streets to take the bus back to Washington, or to continue along King back to our starting point, Ramsay House.

A Morning (or Afternoon) at Mount Vernon

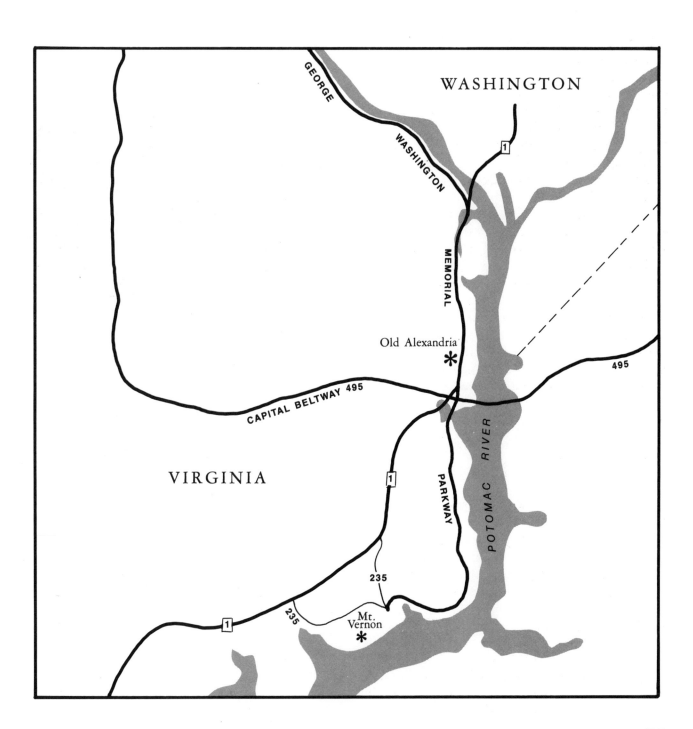

Time: 4–5 hours if you go by bus or boat; 2–3 hours if you go by car. Metrobus: call (202)637-2437 for current bus schedules. Many lines have sightseeing tours, call for information. By car from Washington take George Washington Memorial Parkway south to Mount Vernon Parkway south; or U.S. 1 south to Route 235 south (exit sign Mount Vernon). From the south, take U.S. 1 (Richmond Highway) north to Route 235 (exit sign Mount Vernon). Free parking outside main entrance gate on Route 235. By river, take Wilson line boat at Pier 4, 6th and Water Streets, SW, Washington, D.C. Telephone: (202)554-8000. Round trip fare includes admission. Restaurants: snack bar outside main entrance gate. Mount Vernon Inn is simple but inexpensive. Open daily for breakfast and lunch 8:30–10:30 A.M., 11:30 A.M.–5:30 P.M. No credit cards.

Mount Vernon

Mount Vernon, Virginia. A National Historic Park owned and maintained by the Mount Vernon Ladies' Association. Telephone: (703)780-2000. Open daily: March through October 9:00 A.M.–5:00 P.M., November through February 9:00 A.M.–4:00 P.M. Guided tour. Admission: $4.00 for adults, $3.00 for senior citizens, $1.50 for students and children. Time: 1½ hours.

Seventeen miles south of Washington, **Mount Vernon** is the best-known country house in the United States. Situated on a tree-crowned hilltop overlooking the wide sweep of the Potomac River and the Maryland hills, it presents an idyllic scene of well-proportioned classical buildings set in a landscape of unchanged beauty.

The Washington title to Mount Vernon was part of a grant of 5,000 acres, dating from 1674, to John Washington of Northamptonshire, England, and great-grandfather of George, and Nicholas Spencer. The tract was divided in 1690. The Washington half

Mount Vernon

Paul Hogarth. Mount Vernon

descended by inheritance to Mildred Washington, George's aunt and godmother. In 1726 Augustine Washington, George's father, purchased the tract, then known as the Hunting Creek Plantation, from his sister, Mildred, and her husband, Roger Gregory. In 1735, when George was three years old, Augustine moved from his Pope's Creek estate in Westmoreland County to the Hunting Creek plantation. In 1739 he again moved, this time to Ferry Farm on the Rappahannock River near Fredericksburg. In 1740 Augustine gave the plantation to his son Lawrence, who had just reached the age of twenty-one. Lawrence married in 1743 and settled on the estate, which he renamed Mount Vernon after Admiral Edward ("Old Grog") Vernon, R.N., under whom Lawrence had served in the Caribbean. In 1752 Lawrence died, leaving Mount Vernon to his infant daughter, Sarah. On her death in 1754, George, who had lived with his brother Lawrence since he was sixteen inherited the estate.

During the next five years, military campaigns against the French and the Indians kept the young proprietor away from his plantation. He suffered the horrors of Braddock's defeat and when his health failed him resigned his commission. Life took a turn for the better in 1759 when he married Martha Dandridge Custis, a very rich widow who brought him a dowry of 15,000 acres near Williamsburg, plus 150 slaves. They took up residence at Mount Vernon and the next fifteen years proved to be the happiest of their lives.

Country houses, whether palaces or manors, epitomize history. They are homes as well as works of art. They are not only monuments to but cradles of the great. One might add that there is the house that is the retreat of a great man, and the house that created a great man. Mount Vernon might be described as the house created by a great man. Although begun by Augustine and continued by Lawrence, it was George who gave Mount Vernon its essential character as a classic country estate by making many additions and improvements between 1759 and 1787. The first of these, enlarging the house from one and a half stories to two and a half was made shortly before George's marriage to Martha. Just before the Revolution he also made plans for additions to each end of the mansion; these were not completed until 1787.

The additions were devised, if not designed, by Washington. In Washington's day some knowledge of architecture was an accepted part of a gentleman's education. Though he had been given a practical education as a surveyor, his close relationship with the Fairfaxes enabled him to have access to his lordship's library, which, like that of any other aristocrat of his time, would have included such English architectural portfolios as Colen Campbell's *Vitruvius Britannicus* (London, 1715). His carpenters and masons could do the rest, copying or adapting a pediment or Palladian window, using manuals like Battey Langley's *The City and Country Workman's Treasury of Design* (London, 1741). Washington played, in the eighteenth-century sense, the role of an architect and master builder, one who gathered together the craftsmen needed and undertook all the business transactions, using his distant cousin, Lund Washington, to act as superintendent.

Compared with the larger plantations of the Virginia Tidewater, Mount Vernon is a modest example of colonial country house architecture, which in turn reflects Washington's relatively modest financial status. Yet it is unusually attractive in many ways, perhaps owing more to the harmony of the whole—mansion, outbuildings, and garden—than to the beauty of any individual part. The most striking feature is the high-columned piazza, topped by a gracefully hipped roof and cupola, facing southwest onto the Potomac and extending the full length of the house, a most dramatic adaptation of the Georgian style to an American setting and climate. Another unusual feature is the beveled siding made to resemble stone by sprinkling sand on the freshly painted surface.

During the height of the tourist season you may have to wait in line for 45 minutes or longer; the tour of the mansion itself takes only 25–30 minutes. To the left as you enter is the banquet hall, or "new room" begun under Lund's supervision but not completed until after the Revolution. On each side of the elegantly embellished Palladian window is one of a pair of Hepplewhite-style sideboards made in 1797 by John Aitkin of Philadelphia. The two landscapes of Great Falls and the Potomac at Harper's Ferry and the river scenes above the doors to the little parlor and the west parlor reflect Washington's great interest in the navigable potential of Virginia's river as routes to the West. The former are by George Beck and the latter by William Winstanley. The mantel, which Washington thought too elegant for his republican tastes, was the gift of Samuel Vaughan, an English friend and admirer.

The central hall, or "passage," serves as a vantage point from which you can view the four adjoining rooms, the little parlor, west parlor, downstairs bedchamber, and the dining room. Between the doorways to the dining room hangs the famous Key of the Bastille, a gift from Lafayette in 1790. The barometer beneath the stairs is a reminder of Washington's interest in all that concerned his farm. Through the years he noted the state of the weather in daily diary entries.

The little parlor was used primarily as a music room by Nellie Custis, Washington's stepdaughter. As in any country mansion of the period, music played an important part in the life of Mount Vernon. Gay and spirited social gatherings at which music and dancing were the principal diversions kept both family friends and visitors amused. Washington ordered the harpsichord, which belonged to Nellie, for her from London in 1793. On it is displayed a bound volume of the music she actually played.

Continue to the west parlor, one of the more interesting rooms in the house; the Adam-style ceiling, the doorcases, paneled walls, and the magnificent overmantel make it a superb example of a colonial interior. In the pediment is the Washington family coat of arms. Originally the more important family paintings hung in this room, including the first known portrait of Washington painted during the Revolution. Notice also, the companion pastel portraits of General and Mrs. Washington by James Sharples, a portrait of George Washington by the same artist, and a lively portrait of Mrs. Washington's niece, Fanny Bassett, by Robert Edge Pine.

The dining room, or family dining room, another beautiful room, was built during the autumn of 1775 when Washington faced Boston with his fledgling Continental army.

According to the inventory made by Washington's executors, many of Washington's personal pictures are displayed in this room, including engraved portraits of Franklin and David Rittenhouse. Others include engravings of Washington, Greene, and Lafayette that duplicate those listed in the inventory. The mahogany dining table is an original Mount Vernon piece. The mahogany looking glass that hangs between the windows is another original object in the dining room.

The next room, the downstairs bedroom, a common feature of colonial Virginian homes, may have served as an extra bedroom to house the numerous guests so frequently noted by Washington in his diary.

We now enter the library, completed after Washington left Mount Vernon to attend the second Continental Congress in May 1775. The library bookcases, however, were not installed until some years later. It then became Washington's office, from which he handled the affairs of his 8,000-acre estate. In this room, during the years following the Revolution, Washington directed the establishment of a Federal government. Among the original pieces that remain in the house are a terrestrial globe made in London, a whip stock, a large ducking gun, and a gold-headed walking staff by the desk; all belonged to the great man, as did the ancient iron chest in which he kept his more important documents.

Washington's original library, which numbered more than eight hundred volumes, was left to his nephew, Bushrod Washington, a justice of the Supreme Court. Unfortunately, he divided this priceless collection of books and papers between two of his nephews, George Custis and John Augustine Washington. The civil and military papers were sold to the Federal government just before 1850 and are now in the Library of Congress. A further collection of 350 volumes was acquired by the Boston Athenaeum. By gift or purchase, however, the indefatigable Mount Vernon Ladies' Association has accumulated more than ninety items from the original library.

The last remaining room on the first floor is the pantry, a treasury of chinaware, copper pans, and winechests. Continue now to the rooms on the second floor. These include Nellie Custis's bedroom and General and Mrs. Washington's bedchamber, in which the great man died so unexpectedly during the night of December 14, 1799. The Lafayette room was named for its distinguished occupant, who stayed with the family on several occasions.

Exit from the mansion by the east front. As you leave, pause on the veranda to look at the magnificent view across the river—4,000 acres of forest land protected by scenic easements; the owners have signed agreements to keep the land in its unspoiled natural state.

Adjoining the country house are the courtyard dependencies. The original kitchen is furnished with a motley collection of utensils and devices used to prepare the huge quantities of food served at Mount Vernon. After the Revolution, when Washington was President, the household staff included two cooks and two waiters under the direction of the housekeeper. This staff was always prepared to serve a large number of guests. "My house," Washington once declared, "is like a well-resorted tavern." Washington himself rose at dawn's early light to inspect his estate. Breakfast was at seven. According to the architect Latrobe, a guest in July 1796, this "was served in the usual Virginia style. Tea, Coffee, and cold and broiled meat" served in the sitting room (west parlor?). Lunch was at three, and many guests have left complimentary accounts of the wide choice of fare, which included several wines, beer, and cider. Washington usually remained at the table for an hour, conversing informally with his guests before retiring for a nap. Tea or coffee was served at six, when Washington again engaged guests in conversation before retiring for the night at half past eight. Sometimes supper was served at nine and sometimes not. Latrobe, surprised by the disappearance of his host, as well as the ladies, was left to be conducted by a servant to his own room. "There was no hint of supper," he complained.

Mount Vernon was independent "of everyone but Providence." It grew its own food, had its own mill, shipped tobacco, cotton, and wheat from its own wharf to Alexandria, and kept its own labor force (slaves) in a village of workshops, storehouses, stables, and living quarters in the service lanes to the north and south of the mansion. In 1786, some ninety slaves lived here, constantly employed in an incredible range of tasks, which not only enabled the estate to grow its own food, but also to make its own clothes and shoes. The spinning house on the north lane, the most important building, employed ten or more women to spin and weave wool, flax, or cotton fibers.

The storehouse adjoining the kitchen was used as a depository of tools and supplies issued for the use of and charged to the carpenter, printer, and shoemaker. Three additional buildings, the smokehouse, washhouse, and coachhouse on the south lane, are open to the public. Notice the two-wheeled driving chair, a unique example of a colonial vehicle, which belonged to Washington's old friend and patron Thomas, Lord Fairfax.

From the coachhouse you can walk down to the hollow arched tomb where Washington and his good wife, Martha, lie buried in two white marble coffin-shaped sarcophagi. The one on the left bears the inscription, "Martha, consort of Washington;" the other, simply cut, in massive heavy letters, "Washington."

Continue up the tree-lined path along the Visitor's Approach to the entrance gate, or, if you arrived by boat, return to the wharf.

Washington Tomb

Paul Hogarth has been described as the *chef d'Ecole* of travel art and is famous on both sides of the Atlantic. He was born in Cumbria, England, and in the past decade has drawn America coast-to-coast for *Travel & Leisure*, The National Trust for Historic Preservation, Smithsonian Institution, National Geographic Society, and the London *Sunday Telegraph Magazine*. His own book, *Drawing Architecture: A Creative Approach*, tells how he does it. Other books, notably *America Observed* (with Stephen Spender) and his two previous walking tour books on Boston and Philadelphia, show him to be one of the most important artists recording America's urban and historic heritage today.

He began to explore Washington after his first visit in 1972. Later, he lived in the city for three years with his son, Toby. Mr. Hogarth is currently working on a series of watercolor paintings of the locales of novelist Graham Greene's novels for an album-anthology entitled, *Graham Greene Country*. He is a Royal Academician and is represented in the collections of the Library of Congress, the Boston Public Library, and in England, in the Fitzwilliam Museum and the Tate Gallery.